CB081785

MY CREATIVE JOURNAL

Cambridge Primary Path 1

BY PAUL DRURY

CAMBRIDGE UNIVERSITY PRESS

CAMBRIDGE
UNIVERSITY PRESS & ASSESSMENT

Shaftesbury Road, Cambridge CB2 8EA, United Kingdom
One Liberty Plaza, 20th Floor, New York, NY 10006, USA
477 Williamstown Road, Port Melbourne, VIC 3207, Australia
Torre de los Parques, Colonia Tlacoquemécatl del Valle, Mexico City CP 03200, Mexico
314–321, 3rd Floor, Plot 3, Splendor Forum, Jasola District Centre, New Delhi – 110025, India
103 Penang Road, #05-06/07, Visioncrest Commercial, Singapore 238467

Cambridge University Press & Assessment is a department of the University of Cambridge.

We share the University's mission to contribute to society through the pursuit of education, learning and research at the highest international levels of excellence.

www.cambridge.org
Information on this title: www.cambridge.org/9781108727006

First published 2019

40 39 38 37 36 35 34 33 32 31 30 29 28 27

Printed in Brazil by Forma Certa Grafica Digital LTDA

A catalogue record for this publication is available from the British Library

ISBN 978-1-108-73974-0 Student's Book 1
ISBN 978-1-108-70987-3 Student's Book with Creative Journal 1

Additional resources for this publication at www.cambridge.org/primarypath

VERY SERIOUS INSTRUCTIONS

CONTENTS

THIS IS ME.

Only this person can use this book.

THIS BOOK IS YOURS.

HOW MANY TIMES CAN YOU WRITE YOUR NAME?

Write it BIG.

Write it small.

Write it from top to bottom.

Write it lots of times.

Write it in a different color.

1 WHAT IS A FAMILY?

THIS IS MY FAMILY.

Everyone in my family looks the same as me. Help us look the same. Draw and color.

This is ME!

WHERE'S MY HOUSE?

Match the animal families to their homes. Draw a door on each house.

WHY CAN'T I SLEEP?

Poor stickman. Can you help him sleep?

FINGER-FAMILY

MAKE YOUR FINGER-FAMILY. DRAW AND COLOR.

Do you have a big family?

Add finger-brothers, sisters, uncles, aunts ...

2 WHAT IS SCHOOL LIKE?

THIS IS MY CLASSROOM.

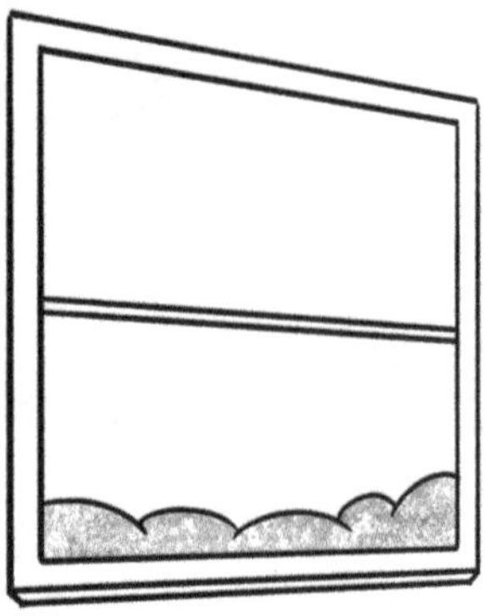

What can your teacher see?
Draw and color.

I WANT TO KNOW EVERYTHING!

Your little brother wants to know lots about school. Write answers to his questions.

What's your teacher's name?

....

Who's the oldest in your class?

....

How many girls are there in your class?

....

How many boys are there in your class?

....

Who do you sit next to?

....

Who's the youngest in your class?

....

What time is recess?

....

What's your favorite thing about school?

....

What do you have for lunch?

....

....

What color is your school bag?

....

Who's your best friend?

....

....

Here's a lollipop. What flavor is it? Give it to your brother.

THIS IS EASY! THIS IS DIFFICULT!

What is easy at school? What is difficult? Write in the chart.

THIS IS EASY!

THIS IS DIFFICULT!

What's easy? Write your ideas here.

What's difficult? Write your ideas here.

ENGLISH

READING

TURN THE BOOK AROUND.

SCIENCE

GYM

What's difficult? Write your ideas here.

What's easy? Write your ideas here.

THIS IS DIFFICULT!

THIS IS EASY!

THE NEW KID

This is the new kid at school. →

He's sad. He has no friends.

Help him make friends.

Draw the new kid playing soccer.

Draw the new kid having lunch.

Draw the new kid having fun.

Can you pass the red, please?

Draw the new kid drawing you.

3 WHAT ARE LIVING THINGS?

SINGING CONTEST

What sounds do these animals make?
Draw the sounds.

Who makes the best sound?

Who is the winner?

Can you make the sounds?

Who is watching? Draw.

BOUNCE, BOUNCE, BOUNCE!

Help the frog cross the river. Spell the names of the insects on the other side.

U	S	E	A	D	B	I	U
V	A	G	P	E	R	U	Z
R	L	O	U	J	A	T	Y
W	T	M	F	G	B	T	D
N	H	J	O	L	T	E	K
K	A	W	P	N	R	N	T
B	Q	H	O	B	F	F	M
I	O	R	T	L	L	X	D
C	M	N	Q	Y	B	Y	F

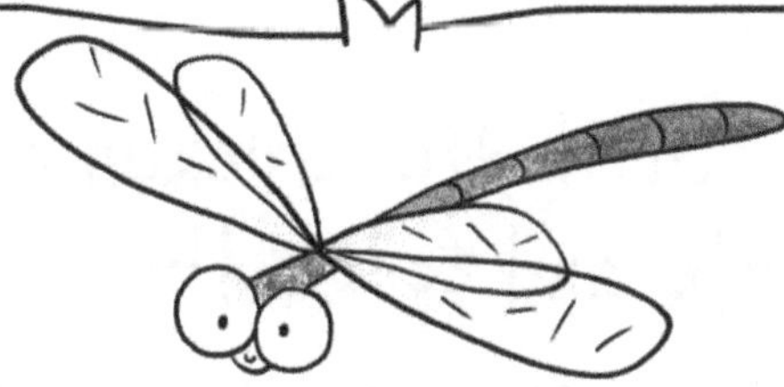

NOT A GOOD DAY

Match the pictures to show what happened to stickman.

What came first: the chicken or the egg?
Complete and color the pattern.

ONE ANT, TWO ANTS...

Ants live in big groups. How many ants can you draw on this leaf?

How many ants are there?

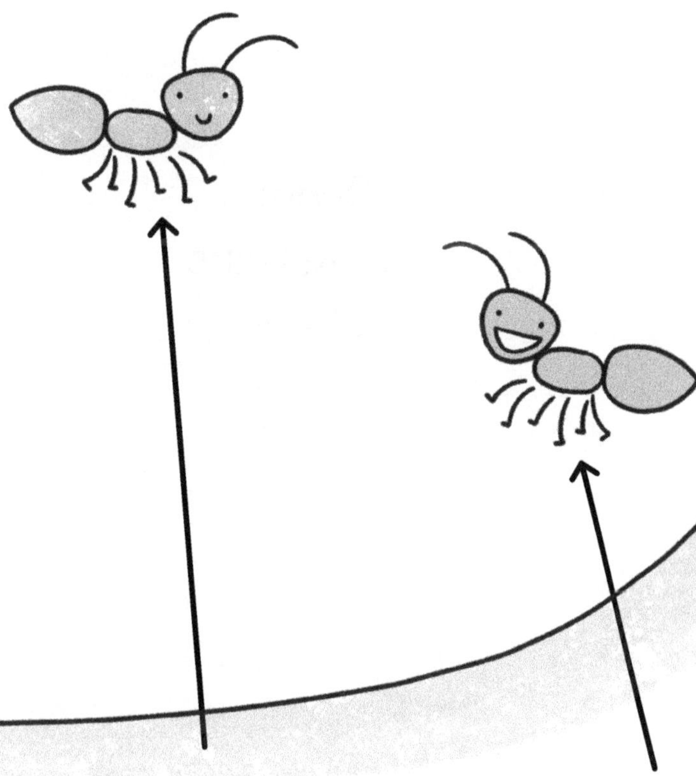

It's spring. Decorate the page with flowers.

This ant is called Bob, and this one is Fred.
What are the other ants called? Give them names.

CREATIVE BLAST 1

FLOW

EVERY SNOWFLAKE IS DIFFERENT.

It's snowing! Draw lots and lots of snowflakes. Remember, every snowflake is different. Use different colors.

Draw a small snowflake.

Draw a snowflake quickly.

Draw a snowflake slowly.

Draw a big snowflake.

Draw a silly snowflake.

FOCUS

WHAT'S IN THE MIRROR?

Look at the pictures.
Draw the mirror image.

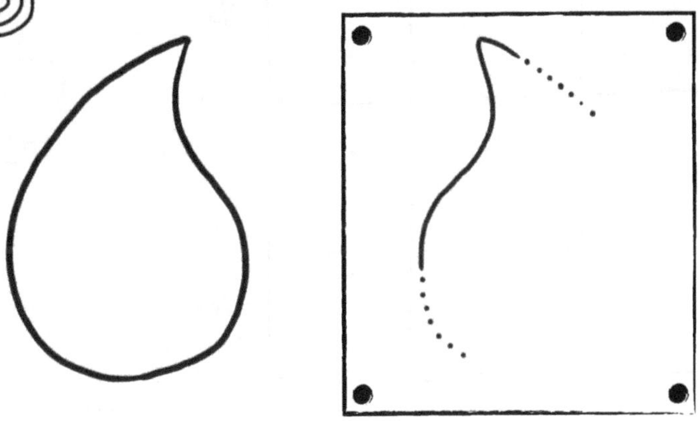

Which shapes are easy to draw?

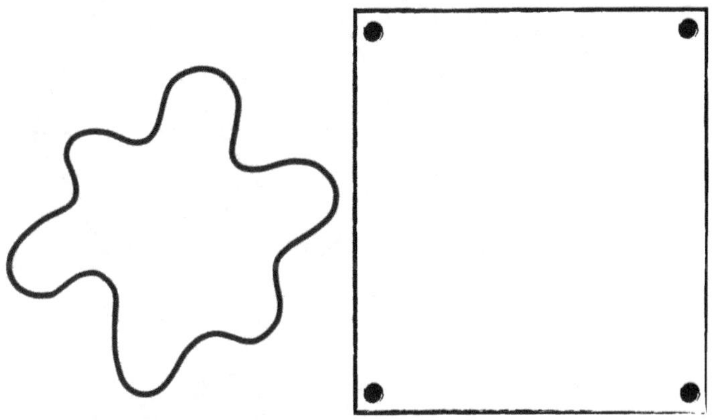

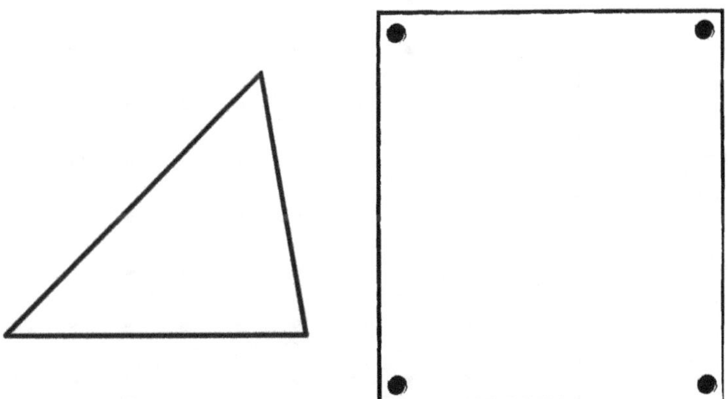

Try using a ruler.

Try using a mirror.

Which shapes are difficult to draw?

4 WHAT IS A FRIEND?

LET'S PLAY!

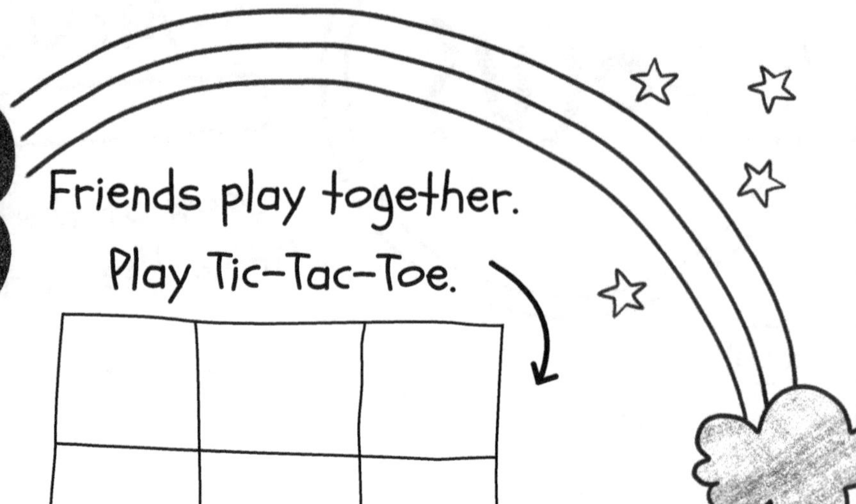

Friends play together.

Play Tic-Tac-Toe.

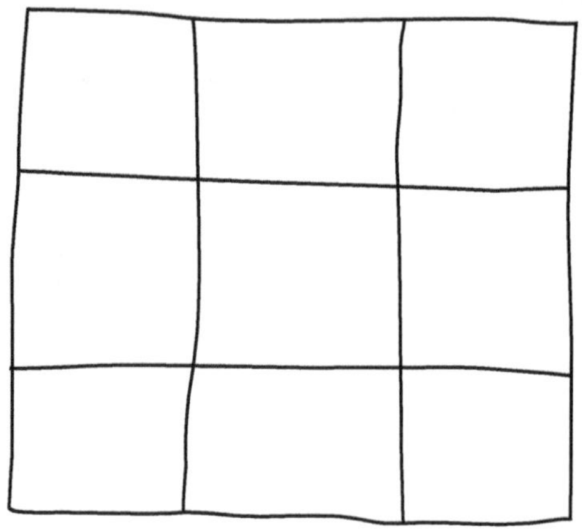

How many triangles can you find?

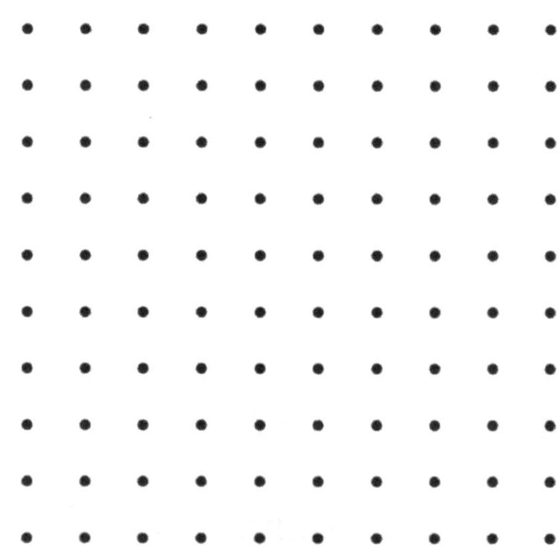

Play Squares.

Take turns to draw one line. If you finish a box, it's yours.

Who can win the most squares?

R S I D G A M T E W N K C

Use the letters to make the words.

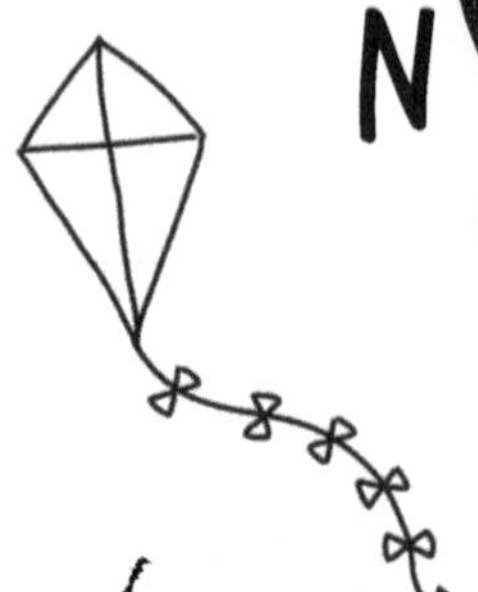

THINGS I DO WITH MY FRIEND

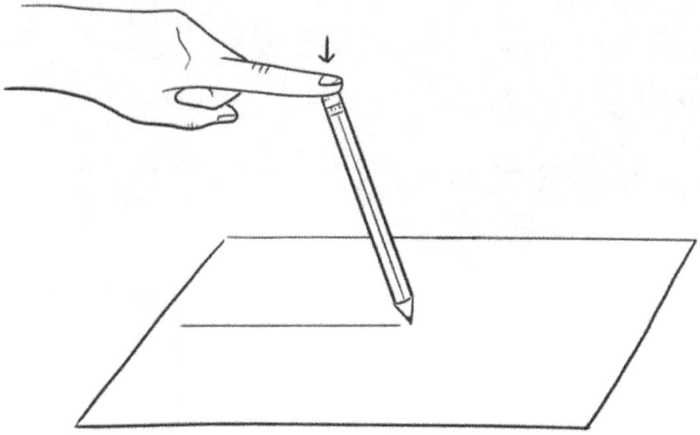

Press down and flick your pencils. Do this to make lines to match the phrases to the pictures.

LET'S... PLAY   LET'S... WATCH   LET'S... GO   LET'S... RIDE   LET'S... VISIT

WRITE A FRIEND POEM

Draw it, think it, write it, glue it, imagine it.

F IS FOR.......................

R IS FOR.......................

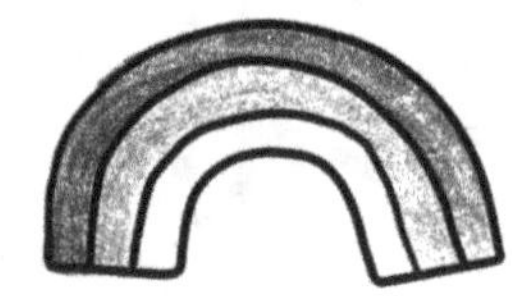

I IS FOR.......................

E IS FOR.......................

N IS FOR.......................

D IS FOR.......................

THESE ARE MY FRIENDS

Oh no! The evil scientist has turned all your friends into shapes!

HERE ARE YOUR FRIENDS! WHO ARE THEY?

Hello

.................................!

This is

....

This is

....

How are you,

.................................?

Give your friends some color!

What do these two numbers like to do together? Draw them having fun!

5 HOW DO WE HAVE FUN?

This is fun!

A DOLL INSIDE A DOLL, INSIDE A DOLL, INSIDE A DOLL …

Decorate the dolls.
Draw more dolls.

WHAT'S FUN?

Draw or glue photos of three things that are fun here.

This is super fun!

This is fun, fun, fun!

What isn't fun? Put a picture here.

How many dolls are there in total?

UP AND DOWN AROUND AND AROUND

WHAT DO YOU KNOW ABOUT THE YO-YO?

This is someone who is good with the yo-yo.

This is me. I'm not good with the yo-yo.

Can you do any tricks? Can you show me? Does your mom or dad know any yo-yo tricks?

Some people think this is how the yo-yo was invented.

The word 'yo-yo' means 'come-come'. How do you say 'yo-yo' in your language? How do you say 'come-come'?

Find a yo-yo and learn some tricks.

Complete the train tracks with words from the unit.

Where is the train going? Draw the place here.

6 HOW CAN WE HELP?

HOW MANY PEOPLE CAN I HELP?

DRAW ALL THE PEOPLE YOU HELP.

Who do you help at home? What do you do?

MY BROTHER

If you help somebody twice, you can draw them twice as well.

Who do you help at school? What do you do?

Remember, they're happy because you help them.

Do you help anyone in other places?
Maybe in the street? In a store? What do you do?

HOW MANY PEOPLE HELP YOU?

DRAW ALL THE PEOPLE WHO HELP YOU.

Who helps you at home? What do they do?

....

Who helps you at school? What do they do?

....

Who else helps you? What do they do?

....

DO YOU SAY 'THANK YOU'?

How many times can you write 'thank you' in this box?

BUSY STICK PEOPLE

The stick people are busy, but they need some help.
Can you give them what they need?

THE CAT'S STUCK IN THE TREE!

Help the cat come down.
Make a tower for the cat.
Use the objects below.

Can you reach the cat?

CREATIVE BLAST 2

TRY, TRY AGAIN

MEMORY TEST

1. Look at all the objects on this page for 1 minute.
2. Now, cover the page with paper.

Count the objects.

Put the objects into groups.

Look for the teddy bear!

Find the ice cream. What's next to it?

3. Which objects do you remember?
Write them here.

4. Look at the page again. How many objects did you remember?

5. Try again. Did you do better?

A DIFFERENT POINT OF VIEW

Look at what the girl is wearing. Draw what's on the back.

7 WHY DO WE NEED PLANTS AND ANIMALS?

SEE THE WORLD LIKE A BAT...

Here are some of the words from the unit. Can you write them upside down?

CHEESE JAM BREATHE BROCCOLI LETTUCE

....

CHEESE

....

What does the world look like to a bat?
Draw this picture upside down.

Can you write the page number upside down? Turn the book around and check.

HANG IT UP TO DRY!

Oh, no! All the words are wet. Can you hang them up to dry?

EGG CAVE HIVE BEANS SEE CLOTH FOREST

FLY BASKET BROCCOLI ONION

PULL

WAKE UP CHEESE TREE JAM

SEED PUSH MEAT

SOIL AIR CROP BREATHE PEPPER LETTUCE

SPINACH

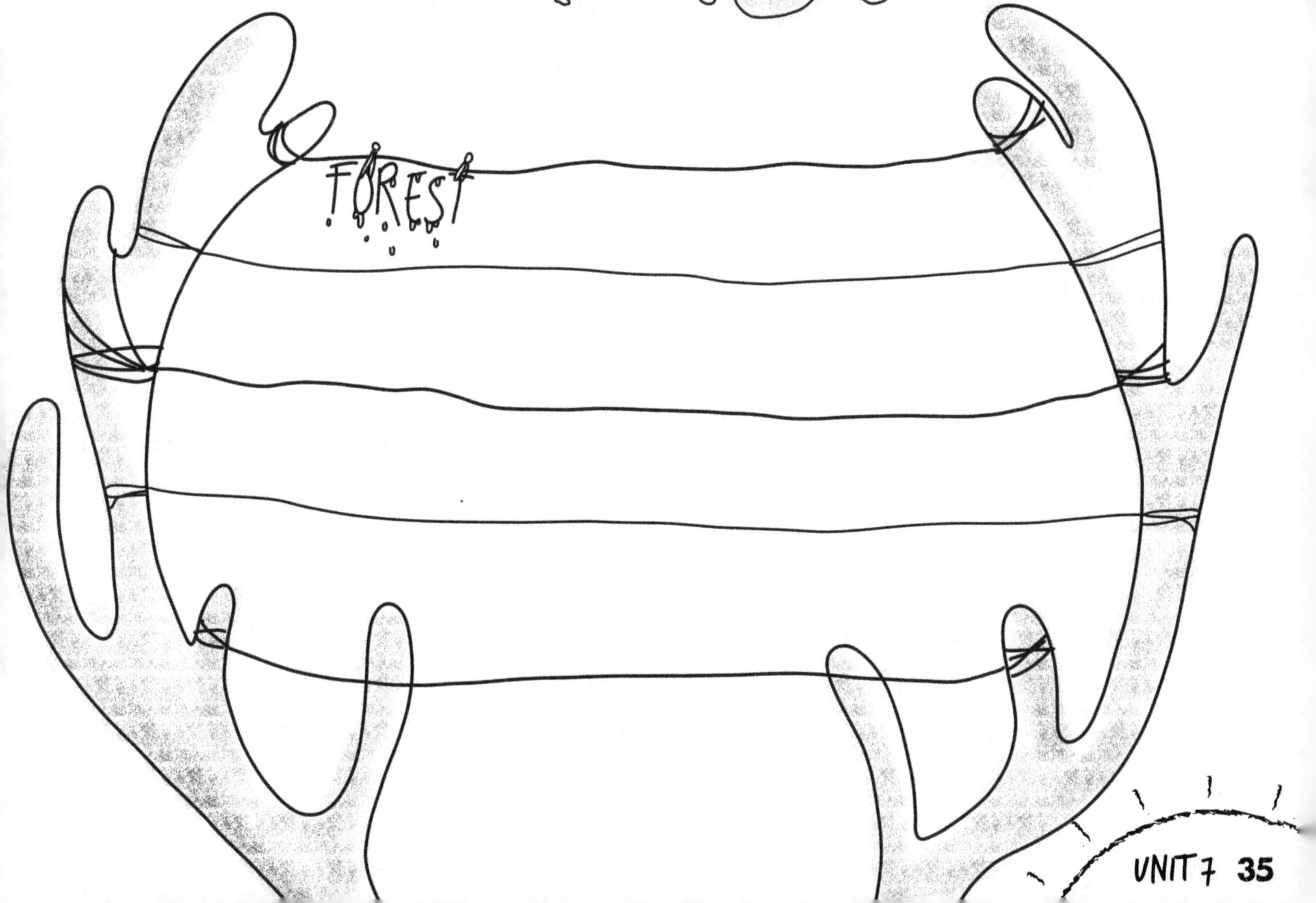

THEY'RE GREEN, THEY HAVE LEAVES, AND THEY'RE EVERYWHERE.

There are plants everywhere. Plants help us in different ways.

We can eat plants.

No, not a house plant. What plants can stickman eat?

Need clothes? Wear a plant.

No, not any plant. What plants can we use to make clothes?

Want to make your house look pretty? Here's a plant.

♫ THE DANCING COW ♩ ♪

This cow wants to dance. Follow the grass to the dance floor.

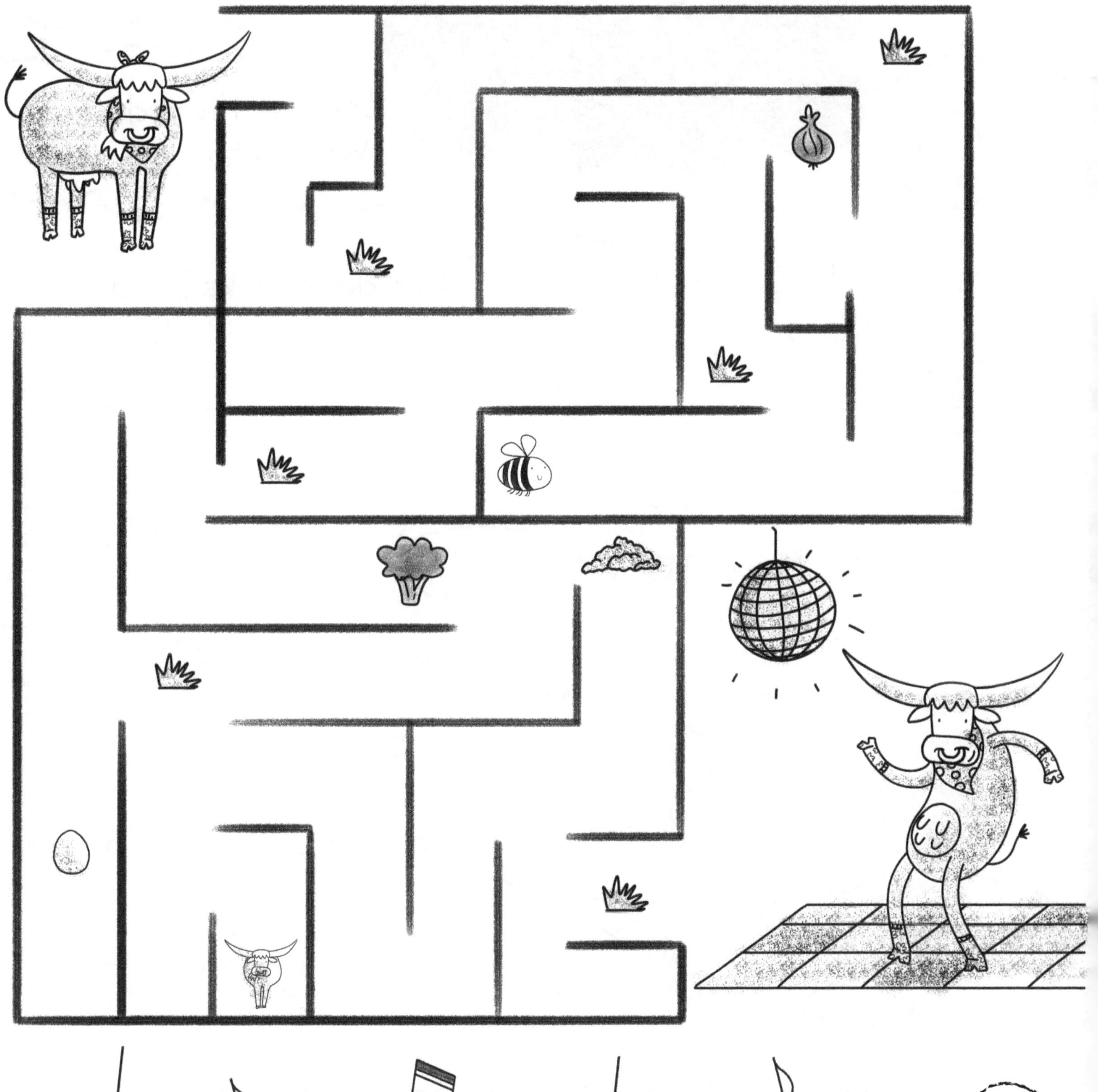

8 WHAT IS IMAGINATION?

IN THE CLOUDS

Look at these clouds.
Write what you see.

This cloud looks like a ...

....

This cloud looks like a ...

....

This cloud looks like a ...

....

Look up at the sky. Look at the clouds or the stars.
What do you see?

IMAGINE THIS

Here are four activities ... have fun!

Decorate this space. Use lots of colors and shapes. Make it amazing!

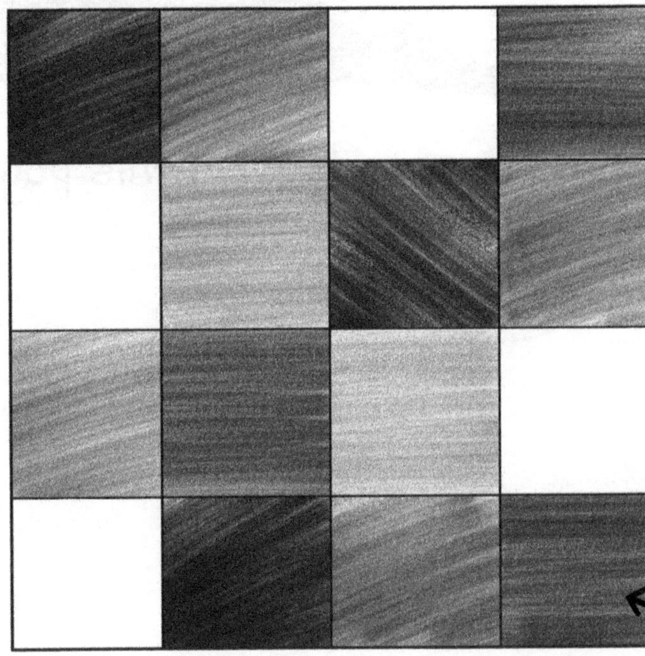

Here's a dance floor! Play some music. Dance with your fingers.

Look for a rainbow. Draw it here. If you can't find one, use your imagination.

Close your eyes. You're on vacation in China. Draw something you buy.

THIS IS YOUR PAGE ...

What does your imagination look like?
Draw it here.

What can you do with this page?
Imagine!

WHAT'S IN THE BOX?

Look! It's a gift for you. But what is it? Answer the questions.

No, it's not a computer, tablet or video game. Too easy!

Is it a living thing?

Is it dangerous?

Is it heavy?

Can you eat it?

Does it make noise?

What color is it?

Is it for children?

What shape is it?

Is it something you can buy in a store?

What's in the box? Draw it here.

9 WHY DO WE NEED CLOTHES?

THESE ANIMALS NEED CLOTHES, TOO!

It's very cold. Give the spider some boots.

It's windy outside. Give the giraffe a scarf.

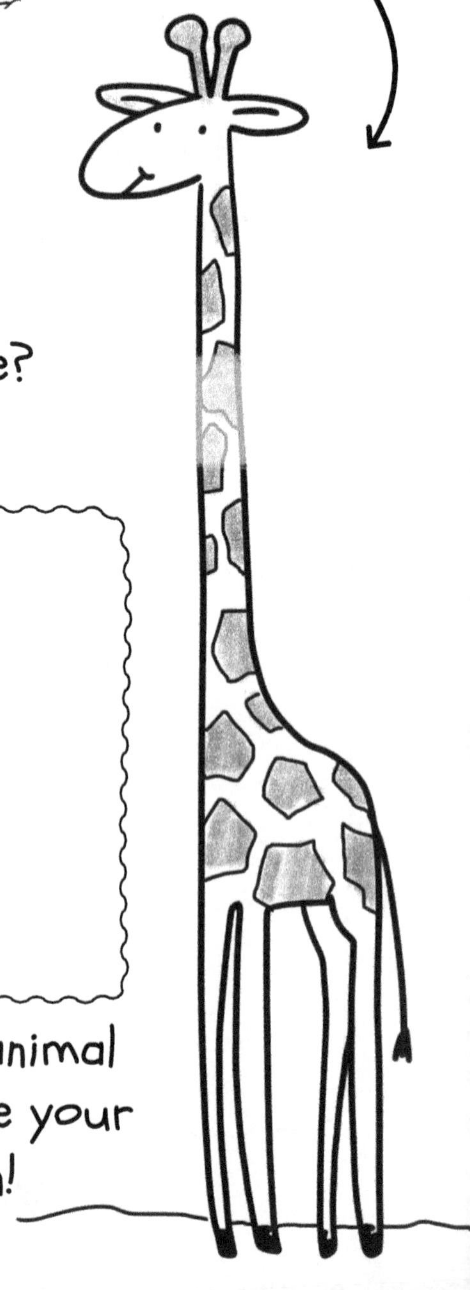

Where does the octopus put its phone? Draw some pockets.

The cat's getting very wet. It needs a hat.

Can you give the cat anything else to keep it dry?

Draw another animal with clothes. Use your imagination!

THE SPECIAL TREE

This tree doesn't grow fruit or leaves. It grows clothes! Draw clothes on the tree.

PARTY CLOTHES

You're going to a party. Wear something really special.
Decorate your party clothes. Color, paint, or glue.

You're going with a friend. Decorate their party clothes as well.

← Decorate the page number for the party.

STAY CLEAN

Go to the party. Don't get your clothes dirty.

It's raining. Don't get wet. Open an umbrella.

Oh, no! Clothes-eating monster! Draw something to get around the monster.

A big hole! Draw or glue something to get over the hole.

The party is up there. Draw a ladder and climb up.

CREATIVE BLAST 3

QUESTIONS, QUESTIONS, QUESTIONS... NEW FRIENDS

Who are the new kids? They have lots of answers. What are the questions? Write them below.

Q: ....

A: Six.

Q: ....

A: English.

Q: ....

....

A: Soccer.

Q: ....

A: Strawberry OK?

Q: ....

....

A: Blue.

Q: ....

A: Yes, I can!

Q: ....

....

A: Going to the movies.

Q: ....

A: Two brothers and one sister.

Can you think of more questions for each answer? What do you want to tell your new friends?

PICK UP A PEN AND DRAW.

Continue the patterns.
Start again if it gets very messy.

It doesn't have to be perfect.

Make very, very big!

You don't like it?
Start again!

THINGS TO REMEMBER

This is you at the start of the year.

You're bigger now. Are you a little bigger or a lot bigger?

This person knows a lot. What's the longest English word you know? Write it here:

....

Can you draw a picture of the word?

What is your favourite activity in this book? Do it again.

Which activity do you not like? Try it one more time.

Cambridge Primary Path 1

Student's Book

Aída Berber

CAMBRIDGE
UNIVERSITY PRESS

LEVEL I: Scope and Sequence

1 Big Question: What is a family?

Reading	Vocabulary	Grammar
Nonfiction *Families Around the World* **Reading Strategy** Predicting from Pictures **Fiction** *Timmy's Family* **Reading Strategy** Identifying Setting	**Key Words 1:** father, brother, mother, sister, grandfather, grandmother **Key Words 2:** family, parents, house, backyard, apartment, grandparents, chore **Key Words 3:** tent, evening **Key Words 4:** aunt, uncle, cousin, bedtime, pajamas, sleep	**Verb *to be*, Affirmative and Negative** I'm seven years old. She's from Colombia. I'm not eight years old. She isn't from Canada. They're from Mongolia. They aren't from Japan. **Verb *to be*, *Yes/No* Questions** Is this Mom? Yes, it is. Are these Grandma and Grandpa? No, they aren't.

2 Big Question: What is school like?

Reading	Vocabulary	Grammar
Nonfiction *Welcome to My School!* **Reading Strategy** Understanding the Meaning of Words in Context **Fiction** *New Friends at School* **Reading Strategy** Predicting from Titles	**Key Words 1:** school, classroom, desk, teacher, uniform, classmate **Key Words 2:** music room, gym, art room, computer lab, principal, nurse, cafeteria **Key Words 3:** drawing, snack **Key Words 4:** new, old, reading, writing, math, library	**Demonstrative Pronouns: *this, that, these, those*** This is a desk. That is the auditorium. These are tablets. Those are uniforms. **Possessive Adjectives** My school is big. Your teacher is nice.

3 Big Question: What are living things?

Reading	Vocabulary	Grammar
Nonfiction *Life in a Pond* **Reading Strategy** Predicting from Titles and Subtitles **Fiction** *Pinocchio* **Reading Strategy** Cause and Effect	**Key Words 1:** grass, flower, ant, earthworm, bee, butterfly **Key Words 2:** pond, water lily, mosquito, dragonfly, fish, frog, tadpole **Key Words 3:** tail, helicopter **Key Words 4:** puppet, wood, happy, dirty, clean, sad	***There is, there are*** There is a dragonfly. There are plants. **Prepositions of Place: *in, on, under, next to*** Where is Pinocchio? He's next to the books.

4 Big Question: What is a friend?

Reading	Vocabulary	Grammar
Nonfiction *Friends! Friends! Friends!* **Reading Strategy** Similarities and Differences **Fiction** *The Hare with Many Friends* **Reading Strategy** Beginning, Middle, and End	**Key Words 1:** draw pictures, play soccer, ride bikes, sing songs, read stories, fly kites **Key Words 2:** friend, recess, share, neighbor, park, swing, slide **Key Words 3:** same, homework **Key Words 4:** hare, hound, goat, ram, calf, chipmunk	**Present Simple: Affirmative and Negative** I lend my pencils. I don't ride my bike to school. He plays with me. He doesn't visit his friends. We share our cookies. We don't go to the same school. **Present Simple: *Yes/No* Questions** Does the horse help Henrietta? No, it doesn't. Do hounds run fast? Yes, they do.

5 Big Question: How do we have fun?

Reading	Vocabulary	Grammar
Nonfiction *Matryoshka Dolls* **Reading Strategy** Identifying the Main Idea **Fiction** *A Box Full of Toys!* **Reading Strategy** Identifying Characters	**Key Words 1:** jump rope, listen to music, dance, play games, bake cookies, paint **Key Words 2:** inside, artisan, outside, collect, travel, buy, gift **Key Words 3:** fit, kind **Key Words 4:** tie, pick up, catch, find, make, write	**Present Simple: *like, likes, don't like, doesn't like*** Some children like playing with dolls. Others don't like playing with dolls. My mom likes collecting dolls. My dad doesn't like collecting dolls. **Possessive *'s*** It's Grandma's yo-yo. Patty is Charlie's sister.

Oracy Skill	Phonics	Writing	Listening	The Big Challenge	Speaking Mission
Ground Rules for Working in Groups **Cue Cards:** **1** I don't understand. **2** Can you repeat that?	**Short *a***	**Learn to Write** Basic Capitalization **Writing Task** You and Your Family	**Interview** Families and Family Activities	**How can we make a photo album?**	**Giving a Home Tour and Introducing Your Neighbor**

Oracy Skill	Phonics	Writing	Listening	The Big Challenge	Speaking Mission
Taking Turns **Cue Cards:** **3** Whose turn is it? **4** It's my turn. **5** It's your turn.	**Short *i***	**Learn to Write** Question Marks **Writing Task** Questions to Ask a New Student	**Dialogue** School Festival	**How can we make useful objects for our school?**	**Welcoming a New Student at School**

Oracy Skill	Phonics	Writing	Listening	The Big Challenge	Oracy Task
Listening to Others **Cue Cards:** **6** Look at this. **7** This is ... **8** I see.	**Short *o***	**Learn to Write** Commas **Writing Task** Living Things in a Backyard	**Narration** Needs of Plants	**How can we show the parts of a flower?**	**Discussion** Designing a School Garden

Oracy Skill	Phonics	Writing	Listening	The Big Challenge	Speaking Mission
Giving Opinions **Cue Cards:** **9** I think ... **10** I agree. **11** I disagree.	**Short *e***	**Learn to Write** Capital Letters and Periods **Writing Task** A Friend	**Dialogue** Welcoming the New Student at School	**How can we make new friends?**	**Arranging a Play Date**

Oracy Skill	Phonics	Writing	Listening	The Big Challenge	Speaking Mission
Asking Questions to Understand Better **Cue Cards:** **1** I don't understand. **2** Can you repeat that?	**Short *u***	**Learn to Write** Exclamation Points **Writing Task** Fun Activities	**Narration** Theme Park	**How can we make a new toy?**	**Buying a New Toy**

LEVEL I: Scope and Sequence

6 Big Question: How can we help?

Reading	Vocabulary	Grammar
Nonfiction *Helping Our Community* **Reading Strategy** Identifying Key Details **Fiction** *A Messy Disruption* **Reading Strategy** Understanding Sequence	**Key Words 1:** sweep the floor, make the bed, water the plants, set the table, donate, recycle **Key Words 2:** help, choose, clean up, trash, bring, pet, adopt **Key Words 3:** list, chat **Key Words 4:** tidy, naughty, dig, break, run away, call	**Present Simple: *have*, *has*, Affirmative and Negative** The kids have a project every month. The bird feeder has seeds. The kids don't have projects every week. The bird feeder doesn't have leaves. **Present Simple: *have*, *has*, *Wh-* Questions** What do Tom and Rick have? They have toys. What does Mrs. Todd have? She has a cat.

7 Big Question: Why do we need plants and animals?

Reading	Vocabulary	Grammar
Nonfiction *Amazing Animals* **Reading Strategy** Using Captions **Fiction** Poems: *Mrs. Bee*, *Cows Can't Dance*, *Five Tall Trees*, *All I Need* **Reading Strategy** Visualizing	**Key Words 1:** cheese, eggs, basket, jam, meat, cloth **Key Words 2:** forest, cave, fly, see, push, pull, rest **Key Words 3:** wake up, crop **Key Words 4:** hive, tree, air, breathe, seed, soil	***Can, can't*** Bats can fly. Bats can't see colors very well. **Countable and Uncountable Nouns** a tree, a bee, a cow some honey, some soil

8 Big Question: What is imagination?

Reading	Vocabulary	Grammar
Nonfiction *Animals of Our Imagination* **Reading Strategy** Understanding Sequence **Fiction** *Ling's Paintbrush* **Reading Strategy** Summarizing	**Key Words 1:** painting, paintbrush, sculpture, clay, camera, photograph **Key Words 2:** craft, dream, imagine, tape, glue, let dry, decorate **Key Words 3:** creator, dots **Key Words 4:** take care, hot, tired, full, empty, thirsty	**Present Simple: *want / need*, Affirmative and Negative** She wants an alebrije. She doesn't want a yo-yo. We need newspaper. We don't need plastic. **Present Simple: *want / need*; *Wh-* Questions** What does the boy need? He needs a bed. What do the people want? They want water.

9 Big Question: Why do we need clothes?

Reading	Vocabulary	Grammar
Nonfiction *All Year Long* **Reading Strategy** Text-to-Self Connections **Fiction** *Nasreddin and the Party* **Reading Strategy** Main Idea and Details	**Key Words 1:** clothes, tennis shoes, wear, dress, sweater, jeans **Key Words 2:** sunny, cold, windy, rainy, snowy, gloves, scarf **Key Words 3:** warm, bloom **Key Words 4:** pants, boots, coat, pocket, take off, put on	**Present Progressive: Affirmative and Negative** I'm wearing a sweater. I'm not wearing a scarf. He's wearing a raincoat. He isn't wearing a hat. The children are riding their bikes. The children aren't playing in the park. **Present Progressive: *Yes/No* Questions** Is Nasreddin sitting under a tree? Yes, he is. Are the people at the party dancing? No, they aren't.

Oracy Skill	Phonics	Writing	Listening	The Big Challenge	Oracy Task
Participating in a Discussion **Cue Cards:** **10** I agree. **11** I disagree. **12** Let's ...	**Ending *-s* and *-es***	**Learn to Write** Nouns **Writing Task** Chores	**Dialogue** Cleaning Up After a Picnic	**How can we show ways to help at home?**	**Collaboration** Helping a Family Member

Oracy Skill	Phonics	Writing	Listening	The Big Challenge	Speaking Mission
Projecting Your Voice **Cue Cards:** **7** This is ... **13** Speak up, please.	**End Sounds *-ng*, *-nk*, and *-ck***	**Learn to Write** Verbs **Writing Task** Description	**Presentation** Where Fruits and Vegetables Grow	**How can we show where produce comes from?**	**Buying Vegetables at the Market**

Oracy Skill	Phonics	Writing	Listening	The Big Challenge	Speaking Mission
Standing Up Straight and Speaking Clearly When Giving a Presentation **Cue Cards:** **6** Look at this. **7** This is ...	**Hard and Soft *g*** **Hard and Soft *c***	**Learn to Write** Adjectives **Writing Task** Description of a Picture	**Dialogue** Imagination Game	**How can we show what we imagine?**	**Inviting Friends to a Costume Party**

Oracy Skill	Phonics	Writing	Listening	The Big Challenge	Oracy Task
Giving and Receiving Positive Feedback **Cue Cards:** **14** Great job! **15** Nice ... **16** Thank you!	**Initial *sh*, *ch***	**Learn to Write** Adverbs **Writing Task** How People Are Doing Things	**Dialogue** Packing for a Special Occasion	**How can we choose clothes for different types of weather?**	**Presentation** Choosing Clothes for Different Occasions

1

What is a family?

- Talk about families.
- Discuss the ground rules for oracy.
- Write about you and your family.
- Give a presentation on your family.
- Show your new neighbor your home.

What do the pictures have in common?

What can you see?

Are all families the same?

1.1

Key Words 1

father	sister
brother	grandfather
mother	grandmother

1 1.1 **Watch the video. Circle the correct word.**

a Who has a big family? **Alice** **Nicki**

b Who has a small family? **Alice** **Nicki**

2 1.1 **Watch again. Complete the graphic organizer in the Activity Book.**

AB page 2

Ready to Read: Nonfiction

Reading Strategy: Predicting from Pictures

Pictures help you predict what a text is about.

1 Look and mark ✓ the correct predictions.

a ☐ This book is about a boy and his hamster.
  ☐ This book is about eating carrots.

b ☐ This book is about life in the city.
  ☐ This book is about life on the farm.

c ☐ This book is a story about dinosaurs.
  ☐ This book is about animals on our planet today.

a

b

c

2 Look at the photos on pages 9–10. What do you think the text is about? Circle the answer.

I think it's about …

a **different toys.** b **different families.** c **different schools.**

1.2

Key Words 2

family

parents

house

backyard

apartment

grandparents

chore

1.3

Families Around the World

Every family is different. Let's look at three very different families around the world.

This is Keith. He is six years old. He is from the United States. He lives with his parents and his brother.

They live in a house. The house is not very big, but it has a backyard with a tree house!

After school, the boys play in the park with their dad. Mom gets home in the evening. Then, they all have dinner.

1.4

Families
Around the World

This is Lucia. She is seven years old. She is from Colombia. She lives in an apartment with her grandparents and her mother.

After school, Lucia helps her grandparents with the chores.

Sometimes Lucia plays with her friends in the apartment. Her grandfather plays with them, too!

This is Odval. She is six years old. She is from Mongolia. Mongolia is in Asia.

Odval and her family are nomads. They go from place to place with their animals.

The family lives in a type of tent called a *ger*. It's time to go! Odval and her family take the ger with them.

Think

How is your family different from these families?

Explore the Text

1A

1 Go back to page 8, Activity 2. Was your prediction correct? Circle.

Yes No

2 Mark ✓ the correct answer.

Which child ...	 Keith	 Lucia	 Odval
a has one brother?			
b travels a lot?			
c lives in an apartment?			
d has a tree house in the backyard?			
e has animals?			
f helps with chores?			

3 1.5 Key Words 3 Listen and repeat. Circle the words *tent* and *evening* in the text. Label the pictures.

1

____

2

____

? How big is your family?
My family is small. There is my mother, my sister, and me.

Grammar in Context

Grammar: Verb *to be*, Affirmative and Negative

I'm seven years old.	**I'm not** eight years old.
She's from Colombia.	**She isn't** from Canada.
They're from Mongolia.	**They aren't** from Japan.

I'm = I am
She's = She is
They're = They are
isn't = is not
aren't = are not

1 1.6 **Listen to the chant and match.**

Gala

Tomo and Koji

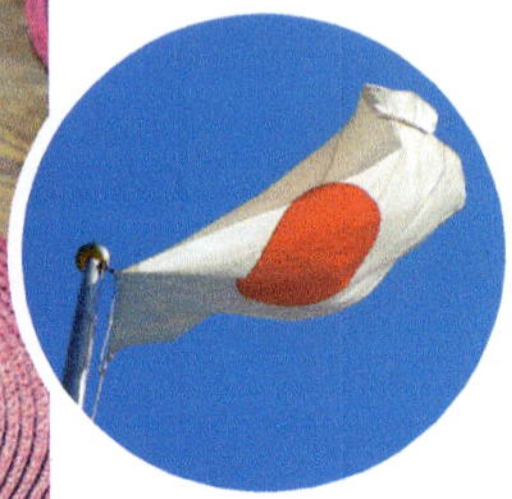

2 **Circle the correct sentences.**

a Gala isn't eight years old.	She is six.	She is seven.
b Gala isn't from Japan.	She is from Colombia.	She is from Brazil.
c Tomo and Koji aren't six years old.	They are eight.	They are seven.
d Tomo and Koji aren't from China.	They are from Brazil.	They are from Japan.

Time to Talk!

Talk to a partner about yourself.
I'm Asli. I'm six years old. I'm from Turkey.

1 1.7 Listen and chant. Mark ✓ what the cat eats.

Pat the Cat
My dad has a cat.
His name is Pat.
His cat is fat.
He likes to eat rats!

2 1.8 Listen and repeat the words with the short *a* sound.

3 1.9 Listen, point, and repeat.

a  ______

b  ______

c  ______

d  ______

4 Label the pictures in Activity 3. Use the words in the box.

bag cap fan bat

5 Play The Word Game. In pairs, say the words quickly. How many times can you say them without making a mistake?

cat, rat, bat, cap, bag, fan ...

Oracy

Oracy Skill: Ground Rules for Working in Groups
Rules help us work in groups.

Oracy Morris

1 **With your teacher, make the rules for working in groups. Use the words in the box.**

respect   listen   take turns   help   share

2 **Write your rules.**

I'm Kate.

I'm Jack.

Ground Rules for Working in Groups

1 We listen ____________.
2 ____________.
3 ____________.
4 ____________.
5 ____________.

I'm Emma.

I'm Liam.

Let's Practice Oracy! I, 2

1. In groups, draw a family tree with the family members from **Oracy Time!**
2. Remember to follow the ground rules.
3. Present your family tree to the class.

Oracy Time!

brother

grandmother

father

grandfather

mother

sister

Check Your Oracy!

1 I followed the ground rules.	Yes / No
2 I participated.	Yes / No

This is our family tree.

This is the father.

Learn to Write: Basic Capitalization

Names of people and countries start with a capital letter.
This is Keith. He is from the United States.

1 Circle the capital letters in the names of people and countries.

a Rick is from Australia.

b Elsa and Vera are from Russia.

2 Rewrite the sentences with capital letters.

a This is alex.

______________________________.

b alex is from argentina.

______________________________.

3 Write about you and your family.

My name is ______________________________.

I am ______________ years old. I'm from ______________________.

I live with ______________________________.

AB pages 9–10

Unit 1B Ready to Read: Fiction

1 1.10 Key Words 4 **Listen, look, and repeat.**

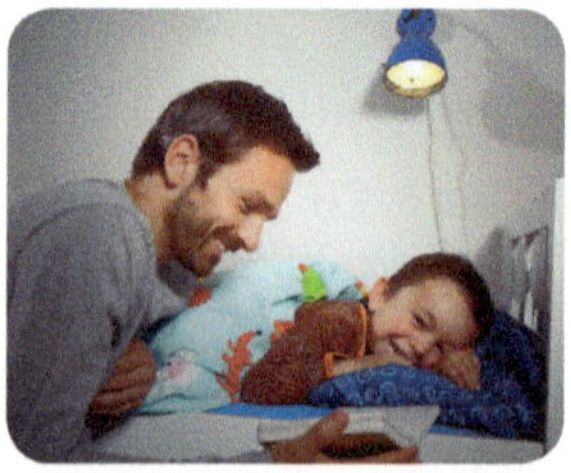

bedtime

pajamas

sleep

2 **Read and circle the correct answers.**

This is a photo of my aunt, my uncle, and my cousins.

a Farid is my **aunt** / **uncle**. He is my father's brother.

b Aysha is my **aunt** / **uncle**.

c My **brothers** / **cousins** are Emir and Rashid.
Emir is twelve years old. Rashid is seven years old.

3 **Complete the sentences.**

pajamas bedtime sleep

a My cousins Rashid and Emir go to ____________ at 8:30 p.m.

b They put on their ____________ and go to bed.

c Every night at ____________, my uncle tells them a story.

Time to Talk!

How many aunts, uncles, and cousins do you have?
I have one aunt, one uncle, and three cousins.

Reading Strategy: Identifying Setting

The setting is the place where the story happens.

1 Read the texts. Look at the pictures. Number the settings.

1 **Will and His Sheep**
Will lives on a farm. He has a cow, a rooster, and a sheep. He loves his sheep!

2 **Snow White and the Seven Dwarfs**
Snow White is a princess. She lives in a small cottage with seven dwarfs.

3 **Grandpa's Houseboat**
Grandpa lives in a houseboat. The houseboat is big!

a cottage

a houseboat

a farm

2 Look at the pictures. Tell a partner which story they belong to.

3 Look at the pictures on pages 18–21. Mark ✓ where you think the story happens.

a at school ☐ b at home ☐

Where do families live?
Some families live in houses.

1.11

Timmy's Family

by Mary C. Brooke

Timmy is not at home.
He is at his aunt and uncle's house.
Grandma is also there.
Timmy's mother and father are on vacation.
Timmy's brother and sister are on vacation, too.

It is bedtime. Timmy is in bed with his toy tiger.
He is wearing his favorite pajamas.
But Timmy is not happy.
He can't sleep.

Think

What can Timmy do to sleep well?

"Are you OK?" asks
Uncle Bob.
"No," says Timmy. "I miss
my mom. I miss my dad. I miss
my sister. I miss my brother.
I can't sleep!"

Grandma has an idea.
"Some warm milk," she says.
Timmy tries it, but he can't
sleep.

Think

What else can Timmy do to sleep well?

1.12 Timmy's Family

Aunt Emma has an idea.
"Some soft music," she says.
Timmy tries it, but he can't sleep.

Timmy's cousin has an idea.
"A bath!" he says.
Timmy tries it, but he can't sleep.

Then Uncle Bob has a
great idea.
"You need your family.
Come with me!" he says.

Think

Are Timmy's uncle, aunt, grandma, and cousin worried about his problem? How do you know?

Back in the bedroom, Uncle Bob draws faces on Timmy's fingers. "Look at your fingers, Timmy."

Timmy looks at his fingers and asks, "Is this Mom?"
"Yes, it is. And this is Dad," says Uncle Bob.
"Is this my sister?" asks Timmy.
"Yes, it is. And this is your brother."

Timmy is happy. "This is Mom. This is Dad. This is my sister and this is my brother," says Timmy.

He slowly closes his eyes.
He sleeps like a baby.

Think

Timmy sleeps well that night. Why?

Explore the Text

1 Circle the setting of the story.

a Timmy's house b Aunt Emma and Uncle Bob's house

2 Read and mark ✓ the correct answer.

a Timmy can't sleep because …

- ☐ the window is open.
- ☐ he misses his family.

b Grandma says …

- ☐ warm milk.
- ☐ orange juice.

c Aunt Emma says …

- ☐ a story.
- ☐ soft music.

d Timmy's cousin says …

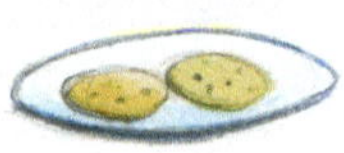

- ☐ cookies.
- ☐ a bath.

e Uncle Bob has an idea! He draws … on Timmy's hand.

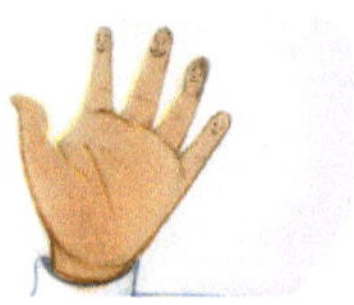

- ☐ Timmy's family
- ☐ animals

f That night, Timmy …

- ☐ can't sleep.
- ☐ sleeps well and is happy.

3 Retell the story with a partner. Use the pictures from Activity 2.

How does your family care for you?
My mother tells me stories. My father plays with me.

Grammar: Verb *to be*, *Yes/No* Questions

Is this Mom? **Yes, it is.** **Are** these Timmy's brother and sister? **Yes, they are.**
Is this Dad? **No, it isn't.** **Are** these Grandma and Grandpa? **No, they aren't.**

1 1.13 **Listen. The girl is talking about her family. Circle the correct answer.**

a Is this Betty's mother? **Yes, it is.** **No, it isn't.**
b Is this her father? **Yes, it is.** **No, it isn't.**
c Are these her cousins? **Yes, they are.** **No, they aren't.**

2 **Look. Mark ✓ the correct answer.**

I'm Jake. This is my family.

a Is this Jake's grandmother? **Yes, it is.** ☐ **No, it isn't.** ☐

b Are these Jake's grandparents?
Yes, they are. ☐ **No, they aren't.** ☐

Time to Talk!

Draw your family. Form groups. Take turns asking and answering questions.
Is this your father? Yes, it is.

Remember your ground rules for working in groups.

1 Look. How many people are there in each family?

2 1.14 Listen and number the pictures.

3 1.15 Listen. Write *Terri*, *Dora*, or *Brad* under each picture.

eating pizza

going to the movies

playing games

Ground Rules for Working in Groups

1 Form groups. Discuss the **Oracy Time!** question.
2 Remember the ground rules.
3 Complete **Check Your Oracy!** in the Activity Book on page 17.

Oracy Time!

What is your favorite family activity?
Playing games.

Values AB page 16

How can we make a photo album?

Your challenge is to take photos of your family and make a photo album.

1. **Take** photos of your family members.
2. **Ask** your parents to help you print the photos.
3. **Bring** the photos to school.
4. **Ask** your teacher to help you fold a sheet of paper to make an album.
5. **Glue** the photos in the album.
6. **Write** captions under the photos: This is my mom.
7. **Present** your photo album to your group.

What is a family?
Look back through the unit. Share your ideas.

AB pages 17–19

SPEAKING MISSION

Give a home tour and introduce your neighbor.

Before Your Mission

1 1.16 **Listen, look, and repeat.**

2 1.16 **Listen again. Mark ✓ your favorite place in the house.**

3 1.17 **Listen and circle. Who is the new neighbor?**

Liu

Mei

Ju

4 1.17 **Listen again. Match the family members with the rooms.**

TV room | **kitchen** | **living room**

Time to Talk!

Where does your family spend the most time at home? Why?
In the kitchen. We eat there. We talk there.

During Your Mission

5 **In pairs, role-play meeting your new neighbor. Give your new neighbor a tour of your house.**

6 **In groups, role-play introducing your neighbor to your family.**

Key Language

Hello! Come in!
I want you to meet my family.
Mom? Dad?
We're in the kitchen.
This is … , our new neighbor.
Nice to meet you.
Nice to meet you, too.
Where's Grandpa?
In the living room.

7 **Draw one activity you can do with your neighbor.**

? **Who can you invite to your home?**
I can invite my school friends.

2 What is school like?

- Talk about places and people at school.
- Learn to take turns in group discussions.
- Write questions for a new student.
- Make recycling bins for paper.
- Welcome a new student to school.

What can you see in the pictures?

Where are the children?

How do you think they feel?

2.1

Key Words 1

school	teacher
classrooom	uniform
desk	classmate

1 ▶ 2.1 **Watch the video. Which school is similar to yours? Mark ✓.**

☐ Jane's school. ☐ Sahil's school.

2 ▶ 2.1 **Watch again. Complete the graphic organizer in the Activity Book.**

AB page 22

Unit 2A Ready to Read: Nonfiction

Reading Strategy: Understanding the Meaning of Words in Context

Some words can give you clues about the meaning of a new word.

1 **Read. Circle the words that help you understand *dull*.**

My pencils are dull. I need a pencil sharpener.

my **pencils** **need** **pencil sharpener**

2 **Mark ✓ the correct picture.**

Dull means …

3 **Read. Circle the words that can help you understand *aprons*.**

In art class, we use aprons to protect our clothes.

Apron means …

4 **Read this sentence from the text on page 31. Circle the words that help you understand *rack*.**

Those are our coats. We hang them on that rack.

Rack means …

2.2

Key Words 2

music room

gym

art room

computer lab

principal

nurse

cafeteria

2.3

Welcome to My School!

I'm Elly. I'm ready for school! Come with me!

Look! This is my classroom. That is me! That is my desk. Those are my classmates. And that is my teacher, Ms. Jones.

Those are our coats. We hang them on that rack.

This is the music room. It is my favorite place! These are the musical instruments we play.

Look! This is the gym. We play basketball here. Ms. Silver is our PE teacher.

This is the art room. Here are all our art supplies, like crayons, colored pencils, and paper. Look at our drawings!

2.4

Welcome to My School!

This is the **computer lab**. We play math and vocabulary games on the computers.

We watch science videos, too. We have lots of fun! These are tablets. We use them often in the computer lab.

Mr. Smith is our **principal**. He is nice to us. He is in his office.

Ms. Wilson is the school **nurse**. This is her office. She gives us medicine and lollipops!

That's the **cafeteria**. We have healthy snacks and drinks there.

I love my school!

Think

Is your school different from Elly's? Why?

1 **Circle *Yes* or *No*.**

a Elly's favorite place at school is the music room. Yes No

b The computers are only for games. Yes No

c The tablets are in the computer lab. Yes No

d The children play video games in the gym. Yes No

e The nurse has lollipops in her office. Yes No

2 **Read and match.**

1	Mr. Smith is	a	our teacher.
2	Ms. Jones is	b	the nurse.
3	Ms. Wilson is	c	the school principal.

3 **Read the sentences from the text on pages 31–32. Circle the words that help you understand *drawings* and *snacks*.**

a This is the art room. Here are all our art supplies, like crayons, colored pencils, and paper. Look at our **drawings**!

b That's the cafeteria. We have **snacks** and drinks there.

4 2.5 Key Words 3 **Listen and repeat. Label the pictures. Use *drawing* or *snacks*.**

1

____

2

____

What's your favorite place in your school?
I like the computer lab.

Grammar in Context

Grammar: Demonstrative Pronouns: *this, that, these, those*

→ This is a desk. These are tablets.

⟶ That is the auditorium. Those are uniforms.

1 2.6 **Listen and number. Then, listen again, point, and repeat.**

2 **Look at Activity 1. Complete the sentences with *This*, *That*, *These*, or *Those*.**

a → ________ is a tablet.

b ⟶ ________ is a computer.

c ⟶ ________ are pencils.

d → ________ are desks.

3 **Complete the sentences with *This*, *That*, *These*, or *Those*. Then, number the pictures.**

1 → ________ is my uniform.

2 ⟶ ________ are computers.

3 → ________ are lollipops.

4 ⟶ ________ is my classroom.

1 2.7 **Listen to the poem and follow.**

Mr. Mill's Mustache

Mr. Mill works at the gym,
He always drinks his milk.
How are you, Mr. Mill?
"I'm fine," he says and grins.
Mr. Mill, what is that?
It's a big milk mustache!

2 2.8 **Listen and repeat the words with the short *i* sound.**

3 **Read and match.**

1 This kid has six figs.
2 Drink your milk.
3 That's a big wig!

a

b

c

4 2.9 **Listen and say the sentences.**

5 **Choose a sentence from Activity 3. Act it out for your classmates to guess.**

Oracy Skill: Taking Turns
When we talk in class, we take turns. We listen to everyone.

Scene 1

Scene 2

1 2.2 2.10 **Watch the video and circle.**

a	Scene 1: Are the children taking turns?	**Yes**	**No**
b	Scene 2: Are the children taking turns?	**Yes**	**No**
c	Which scene is easier to understand?	**Scene 1**	**Scene 2**

Let's Practice Oracy! 3, 4, 5

1. Form pairs. Play the **Oracy Time!** game.
2. Remember to take turns.
3. When you guess correctly, take the object. The student with the most objects wins!

Oracy Time!
Your partner puts a classroom object in a bag. Ask questions to guess the object.

Is it a book?

No. it isn't.

Check Your Oracy!

1 I played the game.	**Yes / No**
2 I took turns.	**Yes / No**

Learn to Write: Question Marks

Questions start with a capital letter and end with a question mark.
Who is this? **Is this your mom?**

1 Underline the questions. Circle the capital letters and the question marks in the questions.

Hi! What's your name?

Grace. And yours?

Greg.
How old are you?

I'm six.

I'm six, too.
Where are you from?

I'm from London.

2 Complete the questions with capital letters and question marks. Match the questions with the answers.

1 ☐ho is this ☐
2 ☐hat is his name ☐
3 ☐ow old is he ☐

a His name is Vince.
b It's my classmate.
c He's seven years old.

3 Write questions to ask the new girl at school. Use the clues.

a What / is / name

____________________________ ☐

b Where / are / from

____________________________ ☐

c How old / are

____________________________ ☐

AB pages 29–30

Unit 2B Ready to Read: Fiction

1 2.11 Key Words 4 **Listen, look, and repeat.**

new

old

reading

writing

math

library

2 **Classify the words.**

School Subjects	Places at School	Words that Describe Objects

3 **Circle the correct answer.**

a In **math** / **writing** class, we play number games.
b In **reading** / **writing** class, the teacher reads stories.
c In **math** / **writing** class, we learn to use capital letters.
d There are many books in the **library** / **gym**.
e My schoolbag is **old** / **new**. It has nice bright colors!

Which do you prefer: writing, reading stories, or doing math problems?
I prefer doing math problems.

Reading Strategy: Predicting from Titles

Titles can help us predict what stories are about.

1 Match the titles with the predictions.

1 "The Sleepy Little Lion"
By Margaret Wise Brown

2 "Flowers for Grandma"
By Mary C. Brooke

3 "Gilberto and the Wind"
By Marie Hall

a I think it's about a boy and his friend the wind.

b I think it's about a baby lion that sleeps a lot.

c I think it's about an old lady who loves flowers.

2 Mark ✓ everything you think will be in the story.

Cow and Rabbit Eat Ice Cream

- a Cow and Rabbit are friends. ☐
- b They have fun. ☐
- c It's in the city. ☐
- d It's on the farm. ☐
- e They eat sandwiches. ☐
- f They eat chocolate ice cream. ☐

3 Look at page 40 and read the title of the story. Mark ✓ what you think it is about.

- a a girl from another country ☐
- b a girl who is new at school and has no friends ☐

Time to Talk!

Form pairs. Say the title of your favorite story. Can your partner predict what it is about?
My favorite story is …

2.12

New Friends at School

by Jeremy Edgar

Jeremy Edgar is from the U.K. He has lived in Mexico for over 35 years. He is an English teacher and author. He also loves reading and riding his motorcycle in the country!

Day 1

I am very, very sad today. I'm the new girl at school. My new school is so big. A lot of students go there, and everyone has friends. Everyone except me! I miss my old school, and I miss my old classmates, too. I even miss my old uniform!

Think

Do you think the girl will feel happy in her new school?

Day 2

My classroom is nice. My new teacher is nice, too. Her name is Ms. Davies. She teaches **reading**, **writing**, and **math**.

Reading is great! The school has a big **library** with lots of wonderful books. I go to the library almost every day.

Math is difficult for me. Luckily, I sit next to Mateo. Mateo is from Peru. He helps me with addition. My new school isn't so bad.

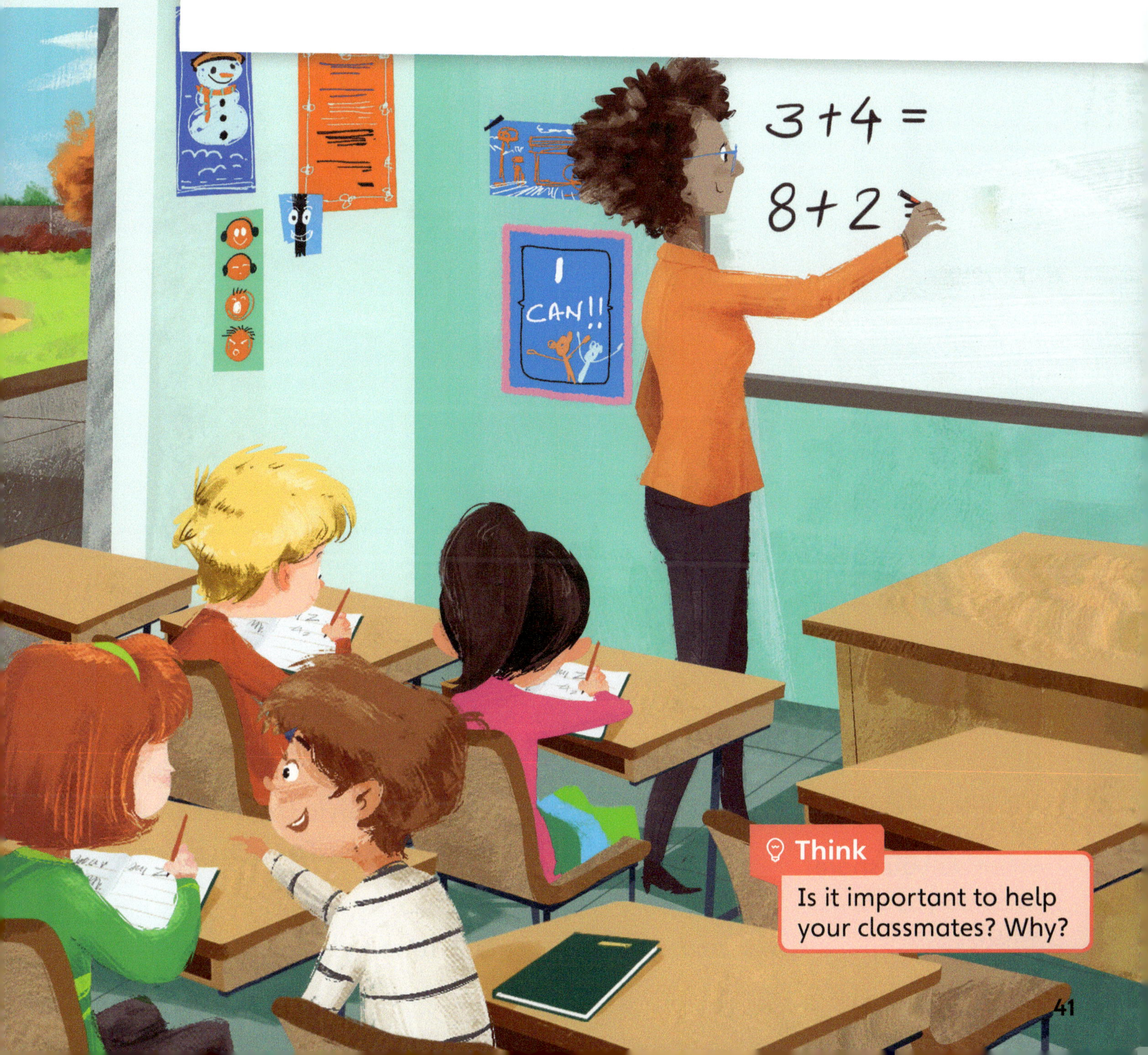

Think

Is it important to help your classmates? Why?

2.13 New Friends at School

Day 3

I love lunch break! Our lunches are different every day. Some of my classmates are from other countries. They bring all kinds of interesting things to eat.

Chen brings fried rice. Her mom is from China. Ivan is from Russia. He brings delicious Russian snacks.

After lunch, we go to the playground. We play hide-and-seek! It's so much fun to play!

Think

Do you share things at school?
What do you share?
Who do you share with?

Think

Why are school friends important?

Day 4

Today is Mateo's birthday party! The party is at his house. Everybody wears nice clothes and eats cake. We are all happy!

School is great! I learn new things and meet lots of new people.

I miss my old friends. But I love my new ones, too!

Explore the Text

1 **Look at your prediction in Activity 3 on page 39. Is it correct? Circle.**

Yes **No**

2 **Mark ✓ the things that Molly does.**

a play on the playground ☐
b go to the library ☐
c invite a classmate to her house ☐
d go to a classmate's birthday party ☐

3 **Circle the correct word.**

a Ms. Davies teaches **math / art**.
b Molly misses her old **school / house.**
c Molly's new school has a big **cafeteria / library**.

4 **Read the sentences and number the pictures.**

1 Everybody has a friend except Molly.
2 Mateo helps Molly with math.
3 Molly plays with her classmates.
4 Molly goes to Mateo's party. She's happy.

5 **In pairs, use the pictures to retell the story.**

What do you do at school?
I play with my classmates.

Grammar: Possessive Adjectives

My school is big. **Your** teacher is nice. **Her** name is Ms. Davies.
His mom is from Mexico. **Our** lunches are different.
Their coats are on the racks.

1 2.14 **Listen and circle the correct words. Who keeps the bag? Circle the correct face.**

My Bag
This is **my** / **your** bag.
No, it isn't.
This is **my** / **your** bag.
No, it isn't!
It's **her** / **his** bag!
It's **his** / **her** bag!

Jane

Tom

2 **Complete the sentences with the words in the box.**

His My your our

a Hi! ______ name is Jess. I'm the new girl at school.
b That is my new friend, Danny. ______ bag is very colorful. I like it very much.
c We love ______ school. It's very big!
d Is ______ school big or small?

3 **Read. Circle the correct answer.**

a Is this her desk? ✓	**Yes, it is.**	**No, it isn't.**
b Are these their tablets? ✗	**Yes, they are.**	**No, they aren't.**
c Is this his lunch box? ✓	**Yes, it is.**	**No, it isn't.**

Time to Talk!

In groups, play **Correct Me!**
My bag is big. No, it's not. Your bag is small!

Remember your ground rules for working in groups.

1 2.15 **Listen and circle the correct answer.**

The school festival is

a **next week.**

b **tomorrow.**

2 2.15 **Listen again and write the numbers.**

	Boys  **Cat Masks**	**Girls**  **Rabbit Masks**
Class 1	______	______
Class 2	______	______
Class 3	______	______

3 **Count and complete. How many masks do you need in your class?**

In my class, we need...

______ cat masks.

______ rabbit masks.

Taking Turns

1 Form groups. Discuss the **Oracy Time!** question.

2 Remember to take turns.

3 Complete **Check Your Oracy!** in the Activity Book on page 37.

Oracy Time!

What is your favorite school festival?

My favorite festival is ...

Values AB page 36

How can we make useful objects for our school?

Your challenge is to make recycling bins for paper for your school.

1. **Form** groups. Each group should bring a cardboard box from home.
2. **Decorate** your box. You can use paints, paintbrushes, paper, glue, or crayons.
3. **Put** recyclable sheets of paper inside your box.
4. **Label** your box: Recyclable Paper.
5. **Present** your box to the class.
6. **Put** the boxes in different places around the school: your classroom, the library, the computer lab, etc.

What is school like?
Look back through the unit. Share your ideas.

AB pages 37–39

SPEAKING MISSION

Welcome the new student at school.

Before Your Mission

1 2.16 **Listen, look, and repeat.**

playground

bathroom

soccer field

teacher's room

science lab

swimming pool

2 **Mark ✓ the places you have in your school.**

3 **Compare your answers with a partner.**

4 2.17 **Listen and circle the correct answers.**

a The new student at school is …

Bruce. **Drew.** **Kim.**

b Recess is after …

math class. **science class.** **English class.**

c Bruce wants to go to the …

bathroom. **gym.** **cafeteria.**

Time to Talk!

Ask a partner questions.

Where is the teacher's room? It's near the science lab.

During Your Mission

5 **In pairs, practice greeting the new student at school.**

Hello!

Are you new at school?

Nice to meet you.

6 **As a class, number the order in which you will show these places to the new student at school.**

soccer field ☐ bathrooms ☐ playground ☐ teacher's room ☐ computer lab ☐ cafeteria ☐

7 2.17 **Listen again. In pairs, role-play the conversation.**

Key Language

Hello!
Are you new at school?
Yes. My name is …
I'm … Nice to meet you.
When is recess?
After math class.
Where is the cafeteria?
It's near the gym.

How do you welcome a new student at school?
I say hello.

3 What are living things?

- ☐ **Talk** about living things.
- ☐ **Learn** to listen and to show you are listening.
- ☐ **Write** about a backyard.
- ☐ **Make** a poster to present the parts of a flower.
- ☐ **Design** a school garden.

What can you see in the pictures?

What do the pictures have in common?

Can you think of other living things?

3.1

Key Words 1

grass	earthworm
flower	bee
ant	butterfly

1 3.1 **Watch the video. Mark ✓ the living things.**

a a flower ☐ b a ball ☐ c an earthworm ☐

2 3.1 **Watch again. Complete the graphic organizer in the Activity Book.**

AB page 42

Ready to Read: Nonfiction

Reading Strategy: Predicting from Titles and Subtitles

The title and subtitles can help you figure out what the text is about.

1 Underline the title in red and the subtitles in blue.

Animals in the Forest

Large Animals

In the forest, there are large animals like bears and deer.

Small Animals

There are small animals. You can find rabbits or squirrels.

Birds

Many birds live in the forest, like eagles or blue jays.

2 Mark ✓ the best prediction about the text in Activity I.

a It's about animals in the forest. ☐

b It's about birds around the world. ☐

3 Read the title and the subtitles on pages 53–54. Mark ✓ the best prediction about the text.

a It's about people in a pond. ☐

b It's about plants and animals in a pond. ☐

3.2

Key Words 2

pond

water lily

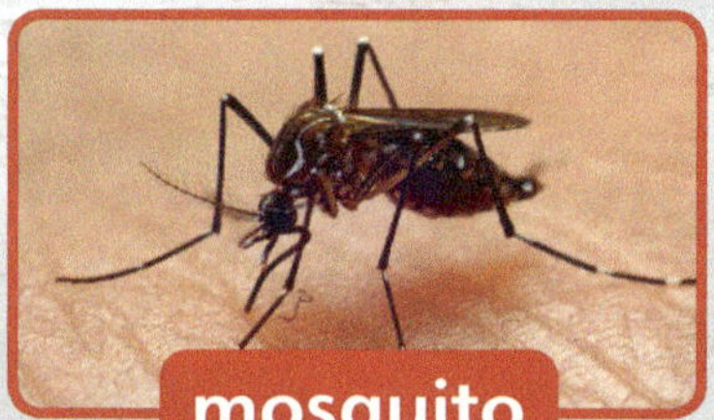
mosquito

dragonfly

fish

frog

tadpole

3.3

Life in a Pond

The Pond

This is a pond. A pond has fresh water. Many animals and plants live here.

Plants

Look! There are flowers in the pond! They are water lilies. They are white.

There are plants all around the pond. Look at this plant. It is a cattail. It is long, and it looks like the tail of a cat!

3.4

Life in a Pond

Animals

There are many insects in the pond. Look!

There are a lot of **mosquitoes**!

This is a **dragonfly**. Dragonflies fly up and down like a helicopter!

This is a water strider. It has very long legs. It walks on the water!

Look! There are two **fish** in the pond. They are called koi. Koi are from Japan. They are orange and white.

There is a **frog** on the rock. And look, these are baby frogs! They are called **tadpoles**.

Think

What else can live in a pond?

Explore the Text

1 **Was your prediction in Activity 3 on page 52 correct? Circle.**

Yes **No**

2 **Read and circle *Yes* or *No*.**

a	There are flowers in a pond.	**Yes**	**No**
b	Some insects live in a pond.	**Yes**	**No**
c	Tadpoles are baby dragonflies.	**Yes**	**No**
d	Koi are fish.	**Yes**	**No**

3 **Read and match.**

Subtitle	Summary
1 The Pond	a There are insects. There are fish.
2 Plants	b A pond has fresh water.
3 Animals	c There is grass. There are water lilies and cattails.

4 3.5 Key Words 3 **Listen and repeat. Circle the words *tail* and *helicopter* in the text. Label the pictures.**

1

____

2

____

Why is water important for living things?
Some animals live in the water.

Grammar in Context

Grammar: *There is, there are*

There is a dragonfly. **There are** plants.

1 3.6 **Listen to the song. What is in this pond? Draw lines.**

2 **Look at the picture of the garden. Complete the sentences with *There is* or *There are*.**

a ________ ______ an earthworm.

b ________ ______ grass.

c ________ ______ flowers.

d ________ ______ ants.

e ________ ______ plants.

f ________ ______ a butterfly.

g ________ ______ a bee near the flowers.

Time to Talk!

Work in pairs. Draw a pond in your notebook. Describe your pond to your partner.

This is a pond. There are butterflies.

Remember to take turns when working in pairs.

1 3.7 **Listen to the chant. Circle the words with the short *o* sound.**

Three Happy Frogs

Bob, the frog, is sitting on a rock.
He's waiting for his friend Ross.
He hears a noise. "Is that you, Ross?"
"No! It's your friend Don!"

Bob and Don are sitting on a rock.
They're waiting for their friend Ross.
They hear a noise. "Is that you, Ross?"
"Yes! It's your friend Ross!"

Now the three happy frogs
Are sitting on a rock!
Are sitting on a rock!
Are sitting on a rock!

2 3.7 **Listen again. Say the words with the short *o* sound.**

3 3.8 **Listen and number.**

1 The pot is hot.
2 The sock is on the clock.
3 My doll is on the floor.

4 3.8 **Listen again and say the sentences.**

Oracy Skill: Listening to Others
When we listen to others, it's good to show that we are paying attention.

1 ▶ 3.2 **Watch the video and circle.**

a	Who listens to Emma?	**Liam**	**Jack**
b	Do you think Emma is happy with Liam?	**Yes**	**No**
c	What does Jack say to show he is listening?	**I see.**	**Wow!**

Let's Practice Oracy! 6, 7, 8

1. Do the **Oracy Time!** task.
2. Form pairs. Take turns describing your drawing.
3. Remember to listen to your partner.

Oracy Time!
Draw three items from nature.

Look at this!

This is my garden.

There is a dragonfly.

Check Your Oracy!

1 I listened.	Yes / No
2 I said "I see" to my partner.	Yes / No

Learn to Write: Commas

We use commas between words in a list.
In the pond there are dragonflies, mosquitoes, and frogs.

1 **Read and circle the commas.**

There are insects like butterflies, ladybugs, and ants in the forest.

2 **Read and add commas.**

There are yellow orange and purple flowers in our backyard!

3 **Complete the text and add commas. Use the words in the box.**

flowers   dragonflies   trees   bees

There are plants like grass ☐ ______________ ☐
and ______________ in my backyard.
There are also insects like butterflies ☐
______________ ☐ and ______________.
I love my backyard!

What other living things are there in a garden?
There are birds.

AB pages 49–50

Unit 3B Ready to Read: Fiction

1 3.9 Key Words 4 **Listen, look, and repeat.**

puppet

wood

happy

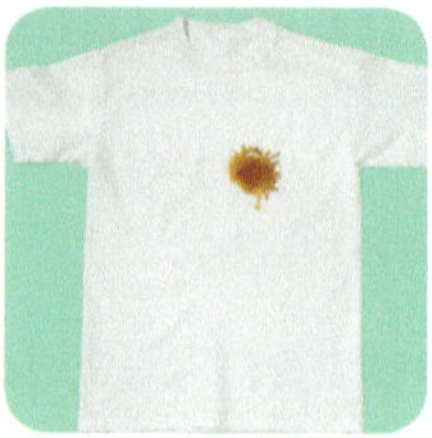
dirty

clean

sad

2 Complete the sentences with words from Activity 1. Then, number the pictures.

1 Dan is a carpenter. Look at the ______________ Dan uses!

2 His shop is not dirty. It is very ______________.

3 Dan is never sad. He is always ______________.

4 He is making a ______________ for a kid!

Time to Talk!

In groups, look around the room. Find something clean, something dirty, and something made of wood.

I can see something clean. Is it the board? No, it isn't. Is it the desk? Yes, it is.

Reading Strategy: Cause and Effect

Effect = what happened   Cause = why it happened

1 **Read. Then, look at the diagram.**

Jack and the Beanstalk

Jack and his mother are poor. Jack sells their cow and gets some beans. Mother is angry. She throws the beans out the window. A big beanstalk grows.

Cause	Effect
Mother throws the beans out the window. 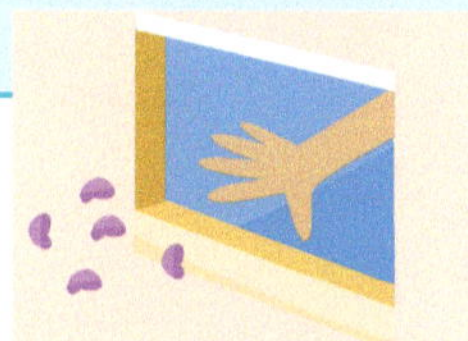	A big beanstalk grows. 

2 **Read. Match the cause with the effect.**

Jack climbs the beanstalk. He sees a castle. A giant and a goose live in the castle. The goose lays golden eggs. The giant is rich because of the golden eggs. Jack takes the goose and escapes. The giant gets angry.

Cause	Effect
1 The goose lays golden eggs. 	a The giant gets angry. 
2 Jack takes the goose. 	b The giant is rich. 

3 **Look at the pictures on pages 62–65. What do you think the story is about?**

What do seeds need to grow?
They need water.

3.10

Pinocchio

C. Collodi's fairy tale adapted by Joep van der Werff

Think

Why is Geppetto happy?

Think

Why does Pinocchio lie to Geppetto?

3.11

Pinocchio

Think

How does Pinocchio feel?

Think

Is the story real or make-believe? How do you know?

Explore the Text

1 **Look and match.**

Cause

1

2

3

Effect

a

b

c

2 **Number the sentences in order.**

- [2] The puppet can move and talk!
- [ ] Pinocchio lies to Geppetto.
- [ ] The books fall on Geppetto.
- [ ] Geppetto sends Pinocchio to school.
- [1] Geppetto, the carpenter, makes a puppet.
- [ ] Pinocchio goes to play.
- [ ] Pinocchio is a real boy!
- [ ] Pinocchio's nose grows.

3 **Form groups. Use the sentences in Activity 2 to retell the story.**

At the end of the story, Pinocchio is a real boy. What can a real boy do?
A real boy can talk.

Remember to show you are listening to your partners.

Grammar: Prepositions of Place: *in*, *on*, *under*, *next to*

Where is Pinocchio? He's next to the books.
Where is the head? It's on the shelf.
Where are the legs? They're under the table.
Where are the books? They're in the bag.

1 3.12 **Complete the questions with *is* or *are*. Listen and circle the correct picture.**

a Where _____ the puppet?

b Where _____ the books?

c Where _____ the schoolbag?

d Where _____ the clothes?

2 **Form pairs. Look at the objects from *Pinocchio*. Ask and answer.**

Where are the legs?

They're on the shelf.

a

b

c

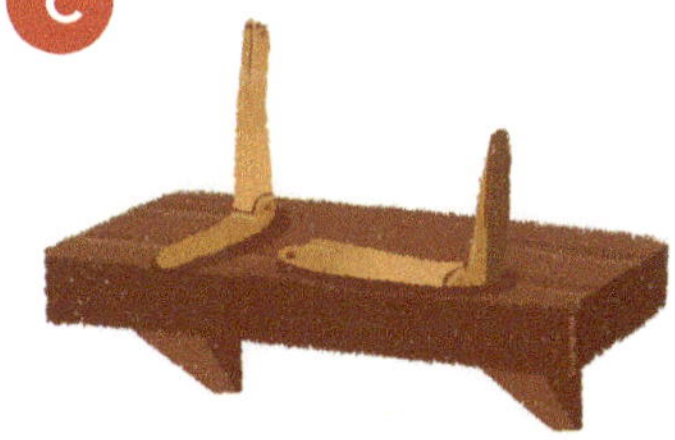

d

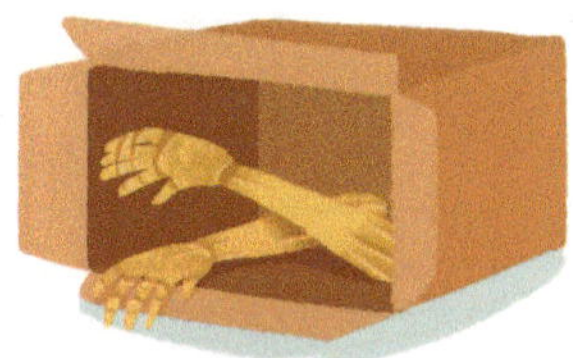

Time to Talk!

Play a game in pairs. Student A hides a pencil.
Student B guesses where it is.
A: Where is the pencil? B: It's under the desk. A: Yes!

1 **Look. Circle the healthy plant.**

a

b

2 3.13 **Listen and mark ✓. Who is talking?**

a teacher ☐ a gardener ☐ a father ☐

3 3.13 **Listen again. Mark ✓ what each plant needs.**

	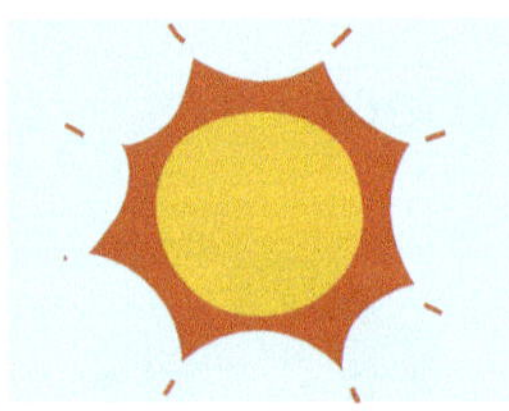 **sunlight**	 **shade**	 **a lot of water**	 **a little water**
 **yucca**				
 **fern**				

Listening to Others

1 Form groups. Discuss the **Oracy Time!** question.

2 Remember to listen.

3 Complete **Check Your Oracy!** in the Activity Book on page 57.

Oracy Time!

What plants do we eat?
We eat lettuce.

Values AB page 56

How can we show the parts of a flower?

Your challenge is to make a poster to show the parts of a flower.

1. **Form** groups.
2. **Draw** and color on a piece of construction paper: an orange flowerpot, a brown square (for the soil), a green stem, two green leaves, five red petals, a yellow circle (for the center of the flower).
3. **Cut out** the flowerpot, the soil, and the parts of the flower. Glue them onto a white sheet of construction paper to make a flower.
4. **Draw** roots on the soil with white chalk.
5. **Label** the parts of the flower: *roots*, *stem*, *leaf*, *petals*.
6. **Present** your flower to the class.

What are living things? Look back through the unit. Share your ideas.

AB pages 57–59

1 Number the pictures.

1 Making Ground Rules for Working in Groups

2 Taking Turns

3 Listening to Others

☐

☐

☐

2 Match the expressions with the skills.

Expressions		Skills
Whose turn is it?	It's my turn.	Listening to Others
Look at this. This is a flower.	I see.	Taking Turns

I want an apple tree in the garden.

YOUR TASK

a You are going to design a school garden.

b Look at the map on page 71.

Trees

apple tree

orange tree

lemon tree

Vegetables

tomatoes

peas

corn

lettuce

potatoes

cucumbers

Flowers

rose

tulip

sunflower

1. Form groups. Discuss what you want in your garden. Mark ✓.
2. Make sure everybody has a turn to talk.
3. Draw a map of the garden on a sheet of paper.
4. Show your garden map to the rest of the class.

Check Your Oracy!

	☺	☺☺	☺☺☺
1 I followed our ground rules.			
2 I took turns.			
3 I listened to everybody.			

4 What is a friend?

- [ ] **Talk** about what a friend is and who are friends.
- [ ] **Learn** how to give your opinion.
- [ ] **Write** about friends.
- [ ] **Give** a presentation on how to make new friends.
- [ ] **Plan** a play date.

Do you think they are friends?

Are the children having fun?

What do you do with your friends?

Key Words 1

draw pictures
play soccer
ride bikes
sing songs
read stories
fly kites

1 4.1 **Watch the video. Mark ✓ the correct answers. Who can be your friend?**

- ☐ your brother or sister
- ☐ a TV character
- ☐ your neighbor

2 4.1 **Watch again. Complete the graphic organizer in the Activity Book.**

AB page 62

Unit 4A

Ready to Read: Nonfiction

Reading Strategy: Similarities and Differences

Finding similarities and differences helps you understand a text better.

~~~~ = *similarities*
~~~~ = *differences*

1 Read the texts. Then, circle *Yes* or *No*.

Jack is six years old. He likes school. He has two friends at school. He plays soccer with his friends. He rides his bike.

Jim is seven years old. He likes school. He has two friends at school. He plays baseball with his friends. He draws pictures.

a	Jack and Jim are both seven years old.	**Yes**	**No**
b	They both have two friends at school.	**Yes**	**No**
c	They both play soccer with their friends.	**Yes**	**No**
d	They both draw pictures.	**Yes**	**No**

2 Read the texts. Underline the similarities in blue and the differences in purple.

Sue is six years old. After school, she goes to the park. She plays on the slides and reads stories.

Tom is seven years old. After school, he goes to the park. He plays on the slides and rides his bike.

3 Look at the photos on pages 75–76. What do you think the text is about?

4.2

Key Words 2

friend

recess

share

neighbor

park

swing

slide

4.3

Friends! Friends! Friends!

My name is Silvia. This is Madison. She's my best **friend**. Having good friends at school is very important. Madison and I do lots of things together. We draw pictures. We read stories. We play during **recess**. We also **share** our cookies during lunchtime. We help each other in the classroom. Sometimes I lend Madison my colored pencils.

Friends! Friends! Friends!

4.4

I'm Patsy, and this is my brother, James. I'm seven, and James is twelve. James plays with me.

He doesn't visit his friends after school. We ride our bikes to many places. Sometimes we go to the park. At home, he helps me with my homework. We are brother and sister, and we are best friends, too.

Hi! I'm Fred. Mike is my best friend. Mike and I don't go to the same school. We are **neighbors**.

We play together after school. We go to the **park** and play on the **swings** and the **slides**. We ride our bikes, too. Sometimes other kids come and play with us!

Think

Who else can be your friend?

1 Match the columns.

1 Silvia and Madison
2 Fred and Mike
3 Patsy and James

a are neighbors.
b are brother and sister. They are friends, too.
c are best friends at school.

2 Read the text again. Mark the table ✓ or ✗.

✓ = *similar*
✗ = *different*

	Silvia and Madison	Fred and Mike	Patsy and James
read stories			
go to the park			
ride bikes			
play during recess			

3 Work with a partner. Which pairs have two similarities in common?

4 4.5 Key Words 3 Listen and repeat. Circle *same* and *homework* in the text. Label the pictures.

1

2

Why are friends important?
We play together.

Grammar: Present Simple, Affirmative and Negative

I **lend** my pencils.	I **don't ride** my bike to school.
He **plays** with me.	He **doesn't visit** his friends.
We **share** our cookies.	We **don't go** to the same school.

1 4.6 **Listen. Mark ✓ or ✗.**

Bill

☐

☐

Jane and Susan

☐

☐

2 **Circle the correct option and number the pictures.**

After school, …

1 I **play / plays** soccer with my friends.

2 she **don't / doesn't** go to the park. She goes back home.

3 he **ride / rides** his bike.

4 we **don't / doesn't** play soccer. We play basketball.

Time to Talk!

What do you do with your friends after school?

I play soccer.

1 4.7 **Listen and sing.**

Friends Help Friends!
Friends help friends.
Friends help friends.
I lend them my pencils.
I lend them my pens.
Friends help friends.
Friends help friends.

2 **Say the words with the short *e* sound.**

3 **Read. Circle the words with the short *e* sound.**

a I lend my pen to my friend.

b My best friend is Ben.

c Ben is ten.

4 **Play with a partner. Choose three words. Say them as fast as you can.**

ten leg pen net

hen nest jet red

Oracy Skill: Giving Opinions
When we give our opinion, we say what we think about something.

1 4.2 4.8 **Watch and circle.**

a	All the children have the same opinion.	**Yes**	**No**
b	It's ok for the children to have different opinions.	**Yes**	**No**

2 4.2 4.8 **Watch again. Circle the phrases you hear.**

I agree. | I think. | I see. | I disagree.

Let's Practice Oracy! 9, 10, 11

1. Form pairs. Give your opinion about the topics in **Oracy Time!**
2. Agree or disagree with your partner.

Check Your Oracy!

1	I gave my opinion.	**Yes / No**
2	I listened to my partner.	**Yes / No**
3	I agreed or disagreed.	**Yes / No**
4	I respected my partner's opinion.	**Yes / No**

Oracy Time!

The best pet.
The best food.
The best sport.
The best toy.

I think soccer is the best sport.

4A

Learn to Write: Capital Letters and Periods

All sentences start with a capital letter.
Some sentences end with a period.
She plays with me.

1 Read. Underline the capital letters and circle the periods.

He is my friend. We go to the park together.

We ride our bikes.

2 Rewrite the sentences. Use capital letters and periods.

a friends are important

______________________ ☐

b the children are friends

______________________ ☐

c they play on the slide

______________________ ☐

3 Write about a friend. Use capital letters and periods.

My friend's name is ____________ ☐

☐*y friend is* ____________ *years old* ☐

We ______________________ *together* ☐

☐*e* ______________________ ☐

☐______________________ ☐

AB pages 69–70

Unit 4B

Ready to Read: Fiction

1 4.9 Key Words 4 **Listen, look, and repeat.**

hare

hound

goat

ram

calf

chipmunk

2 4.10 **Listen and guess the animal.**

I think it's a ram.

I think it's a goat.

3 **Circle the correct word.**

a A **goat / ram** has big horns.

b A **hare / calf** is a baby cow.

c A **ram / horse** is a kind of sheep.

d A **calf / hare** is like a big rabbit.

e A **hound / horse** is a kind of dog.

f A **horse / chipmunk** is small and furry.

4 **Play with a partner. Look at the pictures.**

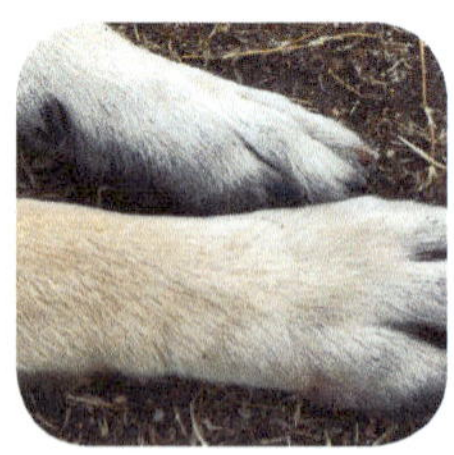

What is it?

It's a ...

Reading Strategy: Beginning, Middle, and End

Every story has a beginning, a middle, and an end.

1 Look at the pictures. Number the parts of the story in order:

1 = the beginning   2 = the middle   3 = the end

☐ The other ducklings don't want to play with the ugly duckling. The ugly duckling swims away.

☐ The eggs hatch, and one duckling looks ugly.

☐ The ugly duckling turns into a beautiful swan.

2 4.11 **Listen and check your answers.**

3 Look at the pictures again. With a partner, read the story out loud in order.

4 Look at the pictures on pages 84–87. Mark ✓ what you think happens in the middle of the story.

☐ ☐ ☐

4.12

The Hare with Many Friends

Aesop's Fable Adapted by Angela Llanas

Angela Llanas is from the U.K. She has lived in Mexico for many years. She has been an English teacher and coordinator. She has written and adapted many stories.

Henrietta is a hare. She is very popular with all the animals. Henrietta is lucky. She has a lot of good friends. Or does she?

What's that noise? Oh, no! It's the hounds! The hounds chase Henrietta! Poor Henrietta! She needs help. She needs a friend!

Think

Who will Henrietta ask for help?

The horse is a good friend. Henrietta runs to the horse. "Help me! Help me! The hounds are after me! Help me, please!" Does the horse help Henrietta? No, it doesn't! The horse says, "Sorry! I'm busy. I'm working on the farm today. Ask the goat!"

The goat is a good friend. Henrietta runs to the goat. "Help me! Help me! The hounds are after me! Help me, please!" But the goat says, "Sorry! Lunchtime! Ask the ram!"

Think

Who can help Henrietta?

The Hare with Many Friends

The ram is a good friend. Henrietta runs to the ram.
"Help me! Help me! The hounds are after me! Help me, please!"
But the ram says, "Sorry! I'm scared of the hounds, too! Ask the calf!"
And the ram runs away as fast as he can!

The calf is a good friend. Henrietta runs to the calf. "Help me! Help me! The hounds are after me! Help me, please!"
"Moo!" says the calf. "I'm very young! I can't help you!"

Think

Are the horse, the goat, the ram, and the calf good friends?
Why or why not?

The hounds are really near now. Where are all of Henrietta's friends? Suddenly, Henrietta sees a chipmunk.
"Please help me! The hounds are after me!"
"Do hounds run fast?" asks the chipmunk.

"Yes, they do!" says Henrietta.
"Hurry! Let's get inside!" says the chipmunk.

Henrietta and the chipmunk go down the hole.

"What a lucky escape! You are a good friend!" says Henrietta.

Think

Who is a good friend in the end?

Explore the Text

1 **Number the pictures in order. Retell the story with a partner.**

2 **Read the sentences. Write *beginning*, *middle*, or *end*.**

a Henrietta goes into a chipmunk hole and escapes from the hounds. ______

b The hounds chase Henrietta. ______

c Henrietta asks her friends for help. ______

3 **Circle *Yes* or *No*.**

a Henrietta asks the goat for help first. **Yes** **No**

b The ram runs away from the hounds. **Yes** **No**

c The chipmunk helps Henrietta. **Yes** **No**

How can you help your friends?
I can listen to them.

Grammar: Present Simple, *Yes/No* Questions

Does the horse **help** Henrietta?	**No, it doesn't.**
Do hounds **run** fast?	**Yes, they do.**

1 4.14 **Listen and circle *Do* or *Does*. Then, write the children's names.**

a **Do / Does** Tim read books? Yes, he does.

b **Do / Does** Tim ride a bike? No, he doesn't.

c **Do / Does** Bob and Tim fly kites? No, they don't.

d **Do / Does** Bob and Tim play tennis? Yes, they do.

____

____

2 **Circle *Do* or *Does*. Then, complete the questions and answers.**

draw ride sing read

a **Do / Does** Julie ______________ a bike? Yes, she ______________.

b **Do / Does** Patrick and Matt ______________ songs? No, they ______________.

c **Do / Does** Bill ______________ stories? Yes, he ______________.

d **Do / Does** Amy and Rose ______________ pictures? No, they ______________.

Time to Talk!

Interview a partner.
Do you ride a bike?
Yes, I do.

Listening

1 Mark ✓ the picture that shows children welcoming the new student at school.

☐   ☐

2 🎧 4.15 Listen and circle the name of the new student at school.

Molly Lynn Sam Ava

3 🎧 4.15 Listen again. Number the pictures in order.

☐ 

☐ 

☐ 

☐ 

Giving Opinions

1 Form groups.
2 Discuss the **Oracy Time!** topic.
3 Remember to agree or disagree.
4 Complete **Check Your Oracy!** in the Activity Book on page 77.

Oracy Time!

We can make new friends at school.

Values AB page 76

How can we make new friends?

Your challenge is to decide the three best ways to make new friends.

1. **Form** small groups.
2. **Look** through the unit and find different things you can do to make new friends.
3. **Draw** three pictures of the different things you can do to make new friends.
4. **Color** the pictures.
5. **Label** the pictures with the names of the activities.
6. **Show** the pictures to the class.
7. **Talk** about the activities.
8. **Decide** on the three best ways to make new friends.

Let's plant a garden. It's a good way to make new friends.

What is a friend?
Look back through the unit. Share your ideas.

AB pages 77–79

SPEAKING MISSION

Arrange a play date. Invite old friends and make new friends.

Before Your Mission

1 4.16 **Listen, look, and repeat.**

watch TV

play on a jungle gym

roller-skate

play hide-and-seek

make modeling clay animals

make a fort

2 **Mark ✓ the things you want to do on the play date.**

3 4.17 **Listen and circle the correct answers.**

a Who is the new kid at school?

Rick Pat Dan

b What are the kids doing on the play date?

Time to Talk!

Discuss with a partner. What do you do on play dates?

We make a fort.

4 Make a list of the old and new friends you want to invite to the play date.

______ ______ ______

______ ______

During Your Mission

5 As a class, brainstorm what you want to do on your play date.

6 In pairs, role-play the conversation.

Key Language

Do you want to come to my house tomorrow?

Let me ask my mom.

Do you like drawing?

Bring your pencils.

Let's invite the new boy!

I'll call him.

How do you make new friends?
I share my things with my new friend.

5

How do we have fun?

- ☐ **Learn** about fun activities.
- ☐ **Ask** questions to understand better.
- ☐ **Write** about fun activities.
- ☐ **Make** a stick puppet and present it to the class.
- ☐ **Play** store and practice buying something.

What can you see?

How do the pictures make you feel?

Do you think the children are having fun?

5.1

Key Words 1

jump rope	play games
listen to music	bake cookies
dance	paint

1 5.1 **Watch the video. Number the activities in order.**

☐ play games ☐ dance ☐ paint ☐ jump rope
☐ bake cookies ☐ listen to music

2 5.1 **Watch again. Complete the graphic organizer in the Activity Book.**

AB page 82

Unit 5A

Ready to Read: Nonfiction

Reading Strategy: Identifying the Main Idea

The main idea is what a text is about.

1 Read. What is the text about? Circle.

There are many kinds of toys, like cars, dolls, balls, and teddy bears. You can play alone or with your friends or family.

The text is about animals.

The text is about toys.

2 Read. Underline the main idea of the text.

Games are fun. You can play them on your own, in pairs, or in groups. For some games, you need special game pieces. To play other games, you don't need anything. You don't need anything to play a guessing game.

a The text is about having fun.

b The text is about games.

c The text is about games you can play on your own.

3 Look at the pictures on pages 97–98. What do you think the text is about?

5.2

Key Words 2

inside

artisan

outside

collect

travel

buy

gift

5.3

Matryoshka Dolls

This is a Matryoshka doll. *Matryoshka* means "little mother" in Russian.

A Matryoshka doll looks like one doll, but when you open it, it has another doll **inside** of it. Then, there is another doll inside of that one. Then another, and another, and another!

Artisans in Russia use wood to make Matryoshka dolls. They make a very small doll first. Then, they make the doll that fits over that one, and then the next one, and the next one, and the next one. They make the **outside** doll last.

5.4

Matryoshka Dolls

Matryoshka dolls have beautiful faces and are very colorful. They are fun to **collect**.

Matryoshka dolls are usually little women.

There are other kinds of Matryoshka dolls. Some of them are animals. You can find dogs, cats, frogs, and even penguins!

Some children like to play with these kinds of dolls.

Some people don't like the animal Matryoshka dolls. They like the traditional ones. When people **travel** to Russia, they sometimes **buy** Matryoshka dolls as **gifts**.

My mom likes to collect Matryoshka dolls. She has twenty big dolls with lots of little dolls inside them!

Think

What games can you play with Matryoshka dolls?

Remember to respect everybody's opinion.

Grammar in Context

Grammar: Simple Present: *like, likes, don't like, doesn't like*

Some children like playing with Matryoshka dolls.
Other children don't like playing with Matryoshka dolls.
My mom likes collecting Matryoshka dolls.
My dad doesn't like collecting Matryoshka dolls.

1 5.6 **Listen to the rap. Match the names with the pictures.**

Hope **Nancy** **James**

a

b

c

2 5.6 **Listen again. Complete with *likes* or *doesn't like*.**

a Hope ____________ jumping rope. She ____________________ dancing.
b Nancy ____________ dancing. She ____________________ playing games.
c James ____________ playing games. He ____________________ jumping rope.

3 **Circle the correct words.**

a I ✗ **like / don't like** jumping rope.
b My best friend ✓ **likes / doesn't like** listening to music.
c Mom ✗ **likes / doesn't like** dancing.
d My classmates ✗ **like / don't like** playing games.

Time to Talk!

In groups, say what you like and don't like doing.
I like listening to music. I don't like jumping rope.

1 5.7 **Listen to the chant. Read and match.**

Bugs and Ducks!

It's so much **fun**
To go to the park
And **run** in the **sun**.

But I just can't stand
The **bugs** and the **ducks**
That make me **jump**.

I feel so scared
That I want to **run**
And get back home!

2 5.8 **Listen and repeat the words with the short *u* sound.**

3 5.9 **Listen and number the pictures. Complete the sentences.**

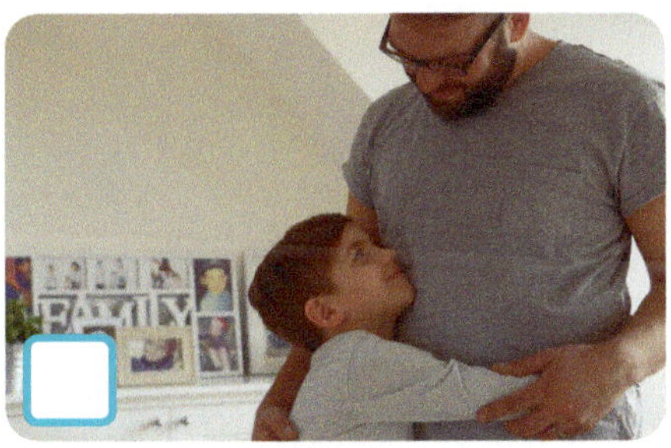

hug

duck

hut

1 Give me a ______________.

2 He lives in a ______________.

3 The ______________ is in the pond.

4 5.9 **Listen again and repeat the sentences.**

The duck is in the pond.

Oracy Skill: Asking Questions to Understand Better
When we don't understand, we can ask questions.

1 5.2 5.10 **Watch the video and circle the correct answers.**

a Do both Liam and Kate understand what Emma says? **Yes** **No**

b Who asks Emma a question to understand better? **Liam** **Kate**

2 5.2 5.10 **Watch again. Circle the phrases you hear.**

I agree. | I don't understand. | Can you repeat that?

Let's Practice Oracy! 1, 2

1. Form pairs. Do the **Oracy Time!** task.
2. Remember to ask questions to understand better.

Oracy Time!

Say random numbers to a partner. Your partner writes the numbers in a notebook.

Can you repeat that?

Check Your Oracy!

1 I listened to my partner.	Yes / No
2 I asked questions when necessary.	Yes / No

Learn to Write: Exclamation Points

We use exclamation points to indicate strong emotions or surprise.
My mom has twenty dolls!

1 Read and number. Circle the exclamation points.

1 We can jump one hundred times!
2 Look at my hands and my face!
3 Let's play video games!
4 I like flying kites!

2 Read. Add a period (.), a question mark (?), or an exclamation point (!).

My friend Laura loves the rain ☐

When it rains, she goes outside ☐

What does she wear ☐

She wears a raincoat and boots.

3 What is the boy saying? Write a sentence. Use an exclamation point.

_______________________________ ☐

AB pages 89–90

Unit 5B Ready to Read: Fiction

1 5.11 Key Words 4 **Listen, look, and repeat.**

tie

pick up

catch

find

make

write

2 Circle the correct word.

Every Sunday, we go to the park.

a My brother and I play baseball. My brother can't **make** / **catch** the ball!

b We run races. Mom always says, "**Tie** / **Find** your shoelaces!"

c We eat lunch. Then, we **find** / **pick up** the trash.

3 Read and complete with words from the box.

find write pick up make

Jordan and her family are at the beach. They have a lot of fun!

1 They ______________ sandcastles.

2 They ______________ shells.

3 They ______________ their names in the sand.

4 They ______________ the trash and keep the beach clean.

? Where can you and your family have fun?
We can have fun at the beach.

Reading Strategy: Identifying Characters

The characters are the people or the animals in a story.

1 **Read. Then, name two more characters in the story.**

The characters are Little Red Riding Hood, the wolf, and ...

Little Red Riding Hood

Little Red Riding Hood visits her grandmother in the woods. A wolf puts the grandmother in the closet. Then, he gets into her bed. The wolf pretends to be the grandmother. A woodsman saves Little Red Riding Hood and her grandmother.

2 **Read *Goldilocks and the Three Bears*. Then, write the characters.**

Goldilocks and the Three Bears

Papa Bear, Mama Bear, and Baby Bear go for a walk. Goldilocks, a little girl, gets into their house. The bears come back home. Goldilocks runs away.

Characters:

____

____

____

____

What is your favorite story?
My favorite story is *Pinocchio*.

3 **Look at the pictures on pages 106–09. Point to the characters in the story.**

5.12

A Box Full of Toys!

by George Baez

Cast of Characters

Narrator — stands to the side of the stage when he or she isn't speaking

Charlie — six-year-old boy

Patty — four-year-old girl, Charlie's sister

Dad — Charlie and Patty's dad

Grandpa Harris

Grandma Harris

Narrator: Charlie and Patty are at their grandpa's house. They see a box in the living room.

Charlie: What is it?

Patty: Wow! It's a box full of toys!

Dad: They are your grandparents' old toys.

Patty: Can we play with them?

Grandma: Sure!

Think

What kind of toys do you think Grandpa and Grandma have in the box?

Narrator: Grandpa looks through the box and pulls out Grandma's yo-yo.

Patty: What is it, Grandpa?

Grandpa: It's Grandma's old yo-yo.

Patty: How does it work?

Grandma: Let me show you. You tie the string to your hand. Then, you roll the yo-yo up and down!

Patty: Wow! This is amazing! Let me try!

Grandma: Sure!

Think

Are old-fashioned toys fun?

5.13

A Box Full of Toys!

Charlie: What's this, Grandpa?

Grandpa: Oh, this is a small rubber ball, of course. These are metal jacks. Jacks is my favorite game. You bounce the ball in the air and pick up all the jacks you can. Then, you catch the ball again.

Charlie: Let's play jacks someday, Grandpa!

Narrator: Charlie finds a crumpled piece of paper.

Charlie: What's this, Grandpa?

Think

What do you think the crumpled piece of paper is?

Grandpa: It's an old paper hat. Let's make two hats, one for you and one for me!

Charlie: But Grandpa, I can't make paper hats!

Grandpa: I can help you. Hold on! Let me show you my favorite toy.

Narrator: Grandpa gets his tablet.

Grandpa: Look, Charlie. I write, "how to make a paper hat." Then, I click on this link. Here's a video. It shows you how to make it.

Charlie: Wow! Your favorite toy is great, Grandpa! I know how to use it!

Grandpa: Fantastic! Then, we can play with my new toy anytime!

Think

What are your favorite toys?

Explore the Text

1 **Go back to the story on pages 106–09. Label the characters.**

2 **Who says what? Match.**

1	"It's a box full of toys!"	a	Grandpa
2	"They are your grandparents' old toys."	b	Charlie
3	"You pick up all the jacks. Then, you catch the ball."	c	Dad
4	"I can't make paper hats!"	d	Grandma
5	"You roll the yo-yo up and down!"	e	Patty

3 **Number the pictures. Retell the story with a partner.**

Do your parents or grandparents still have their toys?
Yes. My grandpa has a toy car.

Remember to ask questions to understand better.

Grammar: Possessive 's

It's Grandma's yo-yo. Patty is Charlie's sister.

1 5.14 **Listen and write *C* (Charlie) or *P* (Patty).**

______ ______ ______ ______

2 Complete the sentences. Whose toys are they?

a It's ____________ toy shopping cart.

b They are ____________ toy cars.

c They are ____________ balls.

d It's ____________ toy tiger.

3 Form pairs. Look and answer. Whose toys are they?

Toy		Vicky	Mark	Helen
	doll	✓	✗	✗
	board game	✗	✓	✗
	teddy bears	✗	✗	✓

Time to Talk!

In groups, ask and answer questions about your things.
Whose pencils are they? They're Tom's pencils.

Listening

1. Look and mark ✓. What is it?

It's a museum. ☐ It's a theme park. ☐

2. 5.15 Listen and circle the name of the park.

Funland **Fun World**

3. 5.15 Listen again. Mark ✓ what you can find in the park.

rides

wild animals

miniature cars

train

games

mini-golf

4. Imagine you are at Fun World. What is your favorite attraction? Number the attractions in order (1–4) starting with your favorite.

games ☐ rides ☐ mini-golf ☐ miniature cars ☐

Asking Questions to Understand Better

1. Form groups. Discuss the **Oracy Time!** question.
2. Remember to ask questions to understand better.
3. Complete **Check Your Oracy!** in the Activity Book on page 97.

Oracy Time!

What do you like doing for fun?
I like playing games.

Values AB page 96

How can we make a new toy?

Your challenge is to make a stick puppet.

1. **Choose** a character from your favorite story.
2. **Draw** the character with colored pencils on a piece of posterboard.
3. **Cut out** the character.
4. **Paste** the character on a wooden stick.
5. **Introduce** your stick puppet to the class.
6. **Play** with your puppet.

This is Harry. He is a character from my favorite book. He is a boy with red hair.

How do we have fun?
Look back through the unit.
Share your ideas.

AB pages 97–99

SPEAKING MISSION

Buy a new toy.

Before Your Mission

1 5.16 **Listen, point, and repeat.**

jigsaw puzzle

stuffed animal

dollhouse

toy train

building blocks

action figure

2 **Look and mark ✓. Which toy would you like to buy?**

3 5.17 **Listen and circle. Which toy do the children want to buy?**

a

jigsaw puzzle
stuffed animal
building blocks

b

toy train
dollhouse
action figure

Time to Talk!

What toys in the pictures do you have?
I have building blocks.

During Your Mission

4 5.17 **Listen again and match.**

How much are the toys?

- $29
- $35
- $39
- $25
- $15

5 In pairs, role-play buying a toy.

Key Language

Can I help you?

Yes. Do you have …?

Here you go.

How much is it? / How much are they?

It's (15) dollars. / They are (20) dollars.

I'll take it. / I'll take them.

Anything else?

No, thank you.

How can you have fun without toys?
I can play with my friends.

6 How can we help?

- Learn how to help.
- Participate in a discussion.
- Write about chores.
- Make a chore chart.
- Suggest ideas to help your family members.

What can you see?

Are the children helping?

Do you do any of these activities?

6.1

Key Words 1

sweep the floor	set the table
make the bed	donate
water the plants	recycle

1 6.1 **Watch the video. Circle the activities you can do to help.**

make the bed **water the plants** **ride your bike**

set the table **sweep the floor**

2 6.1 **Watch again. Complete the graphic organizer in the Activity Book.**

AB page 102

Unit 6A Ready to Read: Nonfiction

Reading Strategy: Identifying Key Details

Key details tell us more about the main idea of a text.

1 Read and match.

At home, we all help with the chores.
My mom sweeps the floor.
My dad washes the dishes. I make my bed.

	Main Idea Family chores	
	Key Details	
1 Dad		a sweeps the floor.
2 Mom		b make my bed.
3 I		c washes the dishes.

2 Read. Write the key details.

There are many things your grandparents and you can do together. You can read stories, play games, listen to music, and even cook!

Main Idea: Activities to do with your grandparents.

You can ______________________.

______________________.

______________________.

______________________.

3 Look at the pictures on pages 119–20. What do you think the text is about?

6.2

Key Words 2

help

choose

clean up

trash

bring

pet

adopt

6.3

Helping Our Community

Hi! I'm Pete. I'm in first grade. In my class, we have a project to **help** the community. A community is a group of people living in the same place. We are all part of a community. Our teacher has a list of places to help. Every month we **choose** a different place.

Sometimes we go to Green Valley Retirement Home. Old people live there.

We play games, read stories, or chat with the residents. We walk with them in the gardens, too.

Other times, we **clean up** the park. We collect **trash**. We pick up bottles, paper, and cans.

6.4

Helping Our Community

We also help nature. For example, we make feeders to help the birds. We put seeds and dried fruit in the bird feeders. We take the feeders home and hang them from branches or windows. The birds come and eat from the feeders.

Today we are at the animal shelter. We always **bring** food and toys for the cats and dogs. We take the small dogs for a walk and play with the cats. Do you have a **pet**? You can **adopt** an animal from the shelter!

Think

What else can you do to help nature?

1 **Circle *Yes* or *No*.**

a Pete's class has a list of places to help. **Yes** **No**

b The children choose three places to help at the same time. **Yes** **No**

c The children help the community and nature. **Yes** **No**

2 **Match the places to the key details.**

1 retirement home
2 park
3 animal shelter

a bring food and toys
b pick up bottles
c chat with the residents
d play with the cats
e read stories
f collect trash

3 6.5 Key Words 3 **Listen and repeat. Number the pictures to match the meaning of *list* and *chat*.**

1 Our teacher has a list of places to help.
2 We chat with the residents.

How can you help your community?
I can visit a retirement home.

Grammar in Context

Grammar: Present Simple: Affirmative and Negative with *have/has*

The kids **have** a project every month.
They **don't have** projects every week.

The bird feeder **has** seeds.
It **doesn't have** leaves.

1 6.6 **Listen and circle what the people have.**

Mr. Allen	Mrs. Clark and Mrs. Reed	Mrs. Smith

tablet / photo album	books / tablet	photo album / tablet

2 In pairs, say what the people have.

Mr. Allen has ...

3 In pairs, say what the children have or don't have. Use words from the box.

bottles cans clothes doll teddy bear car

The boy has some bottles. He doesn't have a teddy bear.

Time to Talk!

Put three things in your schoolbag. In pairs, say what you have.
I have a book. And you? I have a pencil.

1 6.7 **Listen to the chant and follow.**

We're Donating Today!
These are the thing**s**
We're donating today.
Toy**s**, can**s**, blanket**s**, and brush**es**.
Everything is in these brown box**es**.
We'll visit a lot of place**s**.
We're so happy to go!
We'll bring picture**s** to school,
For you, and you, and you!

2 6.8 **Listen and repeat the words ending in *s* or *es*.**

3 6.9 **Listen and number the pictures. Then, check your answers with a partner.**

a

b

c

4 6.9 **Listen again and repeat the sentences.**

5 **Whose bedroom is it? Mark ✓.**

Oracy Skill: Participating in a Discussion
When we participate in a discussion, we listen carefully and respond.

1 ▶ 6.2 🎧 6.10 **Watch the video and circle *Yes* or *No*.**

1. Liam uses *Let's* to make suggestions. **Yes** **No**
2. Jack participates in a discussion. **Yes** **No**
3. Kate always agrees with Liam. **Yes** **No**

2 ▶ 6.2 🎧 6.10 **Watch again. Circle the phrases you hear.**

Let's …	Can you repeat that?	I agree.	This is …	I disagree.

Let's Practice Oracy! 10, 11, 12

1. Discuss the **Oracy Time!** topic.
2. Suggest ideas.
3. Agree or disagree with your classmates.

Oracy Time!

Your friend is sick at home. Discuss ways to help him or her.

Let's call him.

Check Your Oracy!

1 I participated in a discussion.	Yes / No
2 I listened carefully.	Yes / No
3 I agreed or disagreed.	Yes / No

Learn to Write: Nouns

A noun is a person, an animal, a place, or a thing.

The boy cleans up the park.
(person) (place)

We make feeders to help the birds.
(thing) (animal)

1 Underline the nouns. Use different colors.

= person = animal
= place = thing

Grandma is in the backyard.
She loves birds.
She likes to put seeds in the bird feeder.

2 Use the words to complete the text.

cat grandma countryside tablet

This is Bob. He is helping his _______________ (person) use the Internet. Grandma has a new _______________ (thing).

Grandma lives in the _______________ (place).

She needs to buy food online for her _______________ (animal).

3 Look at the picture of the girl. Write a sentence that includes a person, a place, and a thing.

____

____.

AB pages 109–10

Unit 6B

Ready to Read: Fiction

1 6.11 Key Words 4 Listen, look, and repeat.

tidy

naughty

dig

break

run away

call

2 Look and match.

call tidy dig run away naughty break

Time to Talk!

Form groups. Play Charades. Choose a word from Activity 1 and mime it. Your group members try to guess the word.

Reading Strategy: Understanding Sequence

Sequence is the order in which events happen in a story.

1 Read, look, and circle.

a Are the pictures in the correct sequence?

Yes No

Kitty, Come Down!

A kitten is up in the tree. It can't get down! Look! Here are the firefighters. They rescue the kitten. The kitten is safe now.

2 With a partner, number the pictures in Activity 1. Retell the story.

3 Read. Number the pictures in the correct sequence.

The Naughty Wind

Mrs. Clark washes the clothes. Then, she hangs them to dry. She goes back inside the house. A very strong wind comes. It blows, and blows, and blows. The clothes are now on the ground. They are dirty again. Poor Mrs. Clark. She needs to wash the clothes again!

4 Look at the pictures on pages 128–31. What do you think the story is about?

Who helps in your community?
Firefighters.

6.12

A Messy Disruption

By Bodhi Anasha

Tom and Rick are brothers. They always clean their room and pick up their toys together.

"Done!" says Rick.

Both boys are happy when their room is neat and tidy.

Suddenly, a cat comes in through the window.

It jumps onto the bed and plays with the blankets.

"Oh, no, it's Ginger! Ginger is a very naughty cat. And our room is so messy now!"

Ginger is Mrs. Todd's cat. Mrs. Todd is their next-door neighbor.

Think

Why is the cat in Tom and Rick's house?

The boys try to catch Ginger, but they can't.

Ginger jumps onto a flowerpot. He digs up the plants.

He jumps onto the table. He breaks the dishes.

The boys chase Ginger, but he runs away.

He breaks a lamp in the living room. Finally, Ginger hides under the sofa.

Think

Why is the cat running around the house?

6.13

A Messy Disruption

"Here's a ball!" says Tom to Rick.
"Hey, Ginger! Do you want a ball?" asks Rick.
The cat stays put.

"Hey, Ginger! Do you want cheese?" asks Rick.
The cat stays put.

"What can we do?" asks Tom.
"Let's call Mrs. Todd!" says Rick.

Think
Can Mrs. Todd help Tom and Rick?

Mrs. Todd arrives and walks into the living room. "Here, kitty, kitty!" Ginger comes out from under the sofa and jumps into Mrs. Todd's arms.

"Ginger is such a good kitty," Mrs. Todd says. Then, she looks around the house. "Wow! You boys are messy! Clean up before your mom comes home!"

Think

Why does Mrs. Todd say the boys are messy? Is she right?

Explore the Text

1 Circle *Yes* or *No*.

a Tom and Rick are cousins. Yes No

b Their room is always tidy. Yes No

c Ginger is a very naughty cat. Yes No

d Tom and Rick call their parents. Yes No

e Mrs. Todd helps the children clean the house. Yes No

2 Number the pictures in the correct sequence.

3 Work in groups. Use the pictures to retell the story.

What can you do to help your teacher?

We can erase the board.

Grammar in Context

6B

Present Simple: *Wh-* questions with *have/has*

What do Tom and Rick have? They have toys.
What does Mrs. Todd have? She has a cat.

1 6.14 **Listen. Complete the questions and answers. Circle the correct words.**

a 

b 

c 

a What ______ Rose ______? She ______ a broom to **sweep / wash** the floor.

b What ______ Tom ______? He ______ a hose to **water / sweep** the plants.

c What ______ Roy ______? He ______ a rag to **wash / dust** the table.

2 **Work in pairs. Think of things you have in your classroom that you can recycle.**

What do you have?

I have some paper.

3 **Choose and circle three objects for each child.**

4 **Compare your picture with a partner.**

What does the boy in your picture have?

He has a book.

Time to Talk!

What do you have at home that you can donate?
I have some old toys.

Listening

1 6.15 **Listen and mark ✓.**

Where is the family?

2 6.15 **Listen again and match. In pairs, say who does what.**

Mom Dad Bill Julie

Participating in a Discussion

1. Form groups. Discuss the **Oracy Time!** topic.
2. Remember to listen carefully and respond.
3. Agree or disagree with your classmates' ideas.
4. Complete **Check Your Oracy!** in the Activity Book on page 117.

Oracy Time!

Plan a picnic lunch. **We can take sandwiches.**

Values AB page 116

How can we show ways to help at home?

Your challenge is to make a chore chart and to present what you do after a week.

1. **Draw** a chart with the days of the week at the top.
2. **Write** five chores you can do in the left-hand column. For example, make your bed, clean up your bedroom, pick up your toys, and so on.
3. **Keep track** every day. Write a ✓.
4. **Bring** your chart to class after a week.
5. **Present** your chart to the class.

I pick up my toys every day. I set the table on Tuesday and Thursday.

	Monday	Tuesday	Wednesday	Thursday	Friday	Saturday	Sunday
set the table		✓		✓			
clean my room	✓		✓		✓		
pick up my toys	✓	✓	✓	✓	✓	✓	✓
wash the dishes		✓				✓	

How can we help?
Look back through the unit. Share your ideas.

AB pages 117–19

1 What oracy skill are they practicing? Number the pictures.

1 Giving Opinions
2 Asking Questions to Understand Better
3 Participating in a Discussion

☐

☐

☐

2 In pairs, read and match.

1 I don't understand.
2 Let's clean up the park.
3 I think reading is boring.

a I agree. Let's do it!
b I disagree. I think it's fun!
c Can you repeat that?

YOUR TASK

a You are going to think of activities to help a family member.
b Choose ideas on page 137 or think of other ideas with your group.

dry the dishes

push the shopping cart

make dinner

feed the pets

do the gardening

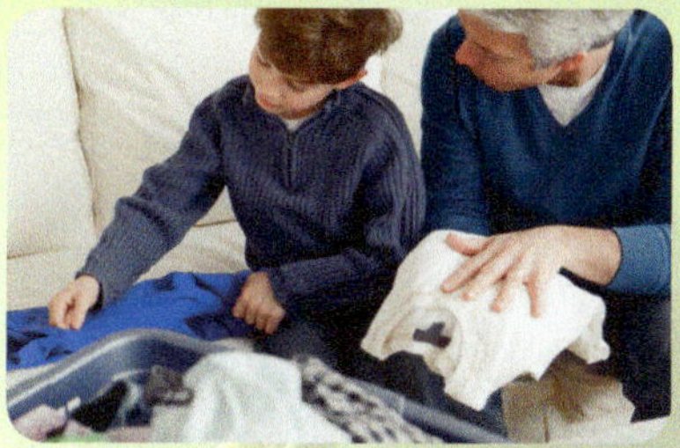

fold the laundry

1. Form groups. Remember your rules for working in groups.
2. Discuss ways you can help a family member. Remember to agree or disagree.
3. Draw pictures of the activities you agree on.
4. Have a group member tell the class what activities you are going to do.

Check Your Oracy!

	☺	☺☺	☺☺☺
1 I participated in a discussion.			
2 I listened to everybody.			
3 I agreed or disagreed.			
4 I asked questions to understand better.			

7 Why do we need plants and animals?

- Talk about plants and animals.
- Learn to project your voice.
- Write descriptions.
- Present where produce comes from.
- Buy vegetables at a market.

What can you see?

Where do these things come from?

What other things come from animals or plants?

7.1

Key Words 1

cheese jam
egg meat
basket cloth

1 7.1 **Watch the video. Mark ✓ the products that come from animals.**

☐ cheese ☐ eggs ☐ basket ☐ jam ☐ meat ☐ cloth

2 7.1 **Watch again. Complete the graphic organizer in the Activity Book.**

AB page 122

Unit 7A Ready to Read: Nonfiction

Reading Strategy: Using Captions

A caption is a sentence under a picture. Captions help us understand the picture and the text.

1 Which photo matches the caption? Mark ✓.

Cows give us milk.

2 Match the captions with the pictures.

1 Cows have horns. 2 A baby cow is called a calf. 3 Cows eat grass.

3 Read. What extra information do you learn from the captions? Circle the answer.

Baby goats are called kids.

Goats are farm animals. They are small and have horns. A mother goat can have two or three kids at the same time.

a Goats have babies.

b The name of baby goats.

Chickens are birds. They live on farms. They eat grass, bugs, fruit, and seeds. Chickens lay eggs.

A chicken can lay 265 eggs per year!

a Chickens lay many eggs.

b Chickens eat grass.

4 Look at the pictures and the captions on pages 141–42. What do you think the text is about?

7.2

Key Words 2

forest

cave

fly

see

push

pull

rest

7.3

Amazing Animals

Bats

Bats are small. They sleep in the day and wake up at night.

Bats sleep upside down.

Bats live in the desert, in the forest, and in the city.

Bats sleep in caves, trees, and in old buildings.

Bats are mammals. They have fur. Baby bats drink milk from their mother.

Bats can fly. They are the only mammals that can fly!

Bats can't see colors very well, so they use their ears. They listen to the echoes to help them fly.

Bats eat fruit, flower nectar, and insects. They eat a lot of insects. A single bat can eat 1,200 mosquitoes in one hour!

Bats eat insects that are bad for crops and gardens. In this way, bats help people.

Stop and think. Bats are important for nature!

Think

Why do people need bats?

7.4

Amazing Animals

Reindeer

Reindeer are big. They live in very cold places. They love the snow!

Reindeer have big antlers. They use their antlers to push the snow and find food.

Reindeer eat plants and grass. Their favorite food is green leaves.

Reindeer have hard hooves to walk on the snow and on the ice. They also have thick fur. This helps them to stay warm.

Wild reindeer in North America are called caribou.

Reindeer help people. They are very strong, and they can pull sleighs. They can run very fast, too. They can run 80 km per hour. That is as fast as a car!

Reindeer are very social creatures. They eat, travel, and rest in groups.

Think

What other animals help people pull heavy things?

1 **Circle the correct animals.**

a	They can fly.	**bats**	**reindeer**
b	They push the snow with their antlers.	**bats**	**reindeer**
c	They sleep upside down.	**bats**	**reindeer**
d	They help control insects.	**bats**	**reindeer**
e	They help pull heavy things.	**bats**	**reindeer**

2 **Look and read. Underline the correct caption for each picture.**

1

a Bats eat flower nectar.

b Bats eat a lot of insects.

2

a Reindeer play in the snow.

b Reindeer pull sleighs.

3 7.5 Key Words 3 **Circle *wake up* and *crops* in the text. Then, read and number the pictures.**

1 I **wake up** at 6:30 every morning.

2 Look at those **crops**! Are they grapes or tomatoes?

What animals help people?
How do they help people?
Horses help people. You can ride them.

Remember to listen carefully and to respond when you participate in a discussion.

Grammar: *can, can't*

Bats can fly. **Bats can't see colors very well.**

1 7.6 **Listen and number the animals in order.**

eagle

hare

chipmunk

2 7.6 **Listen again. Write about what the animals can and can't do.**

hop fly climb run

a Hares can ____________. Hares can't ____________.

b Chipmunks can ____________. Chipmunks can't ____________.

c Eagles can ____________. Eagles can't ____________.

3 **With a partner, talk about the animals.**

Chipmunks can climb.
They can't fly.

Time to Talk!

Talk to your partner about things you can and can't do.
I can draw pictures.
I can't ride a bike.

1 7.7 **Listen, follow, and match.**

The king likes to sing. | Frank wears pink shoes. | Jack has a new trick.

2 **Circle the final consonants in each word.**

clock rock sing wing pink drink

3 7.8 **Listen and repeat the words in Activity 2.**

4 7.9 **Look at the pictures. Listen and circle the words with the same final sound.**

swing / brick

long / black

sink / strong

5 **In pairs, say the tongue twisters. Who can say them faster?**

Frank has a pink skunk.

The king likes to sing on the swing.

Oracy Skill: Projecting Your Voice
When we talk in front of our class, we speak loudly and clearly.

1 7.2 7.10 **Watch the video and circle.**

1

2

In which scene …

a does Jack speak clearly and loudly? 1 2

b can Jack's classmates hear him clearly? 1 2

2 7.2 7.10 **Watch again. Circle the phrases you hear.**

This is … **I think …** **I agree.** **Speak up, please.**

Let's Practice Oracy! 7, 13

1. Do the **Oracy Time!** task.
2. Form groups. Present your favorite fruit or vegetable to your group.
3. Remember to project your voice. Ask your classmates to speak up if you can't hear them.

Oracy Time!

Draw your favorite fruit or vegetable.

This is a pear! It's my favorite fruit.

Check Your Oracy!

1 I used *This is …* to present the information.	Yes / No
2 My classmates asked me to speak up.	Yes / No
3 I spoke clearly and loudly.	Yes / No

Learn to Write: Verbs

A verb is a word for an action or a state of being.
Bears are mammals. (state of being)
They have fur. (state of being)
Bears eat berries and meat. (action)
Bears sleep during the winter. (action)

1 Read and circle the verbs. Are they actions or a state of being?

Camels live in the desert. They have very big feet. Camels run as fast as a horse.

They eat plants from the desert. They give us milk. Camel milk is delicious!

2 Read and circle the correct verbs.

Ants are small. They are very strong. They have six legs. Ants **live** / **fly** in groups called colonies. They **make** / **pull** their own house—an anthill! They **push** / **eat** seeds, nectar, worms, and leaves. Ants are great!

3 Write three sentences to describe the picture.

AB pages 129–30

Unit 7B

Ready to Read: Fiction

1 7.11 **Listen, look, and repeat.**

hive

tree

air

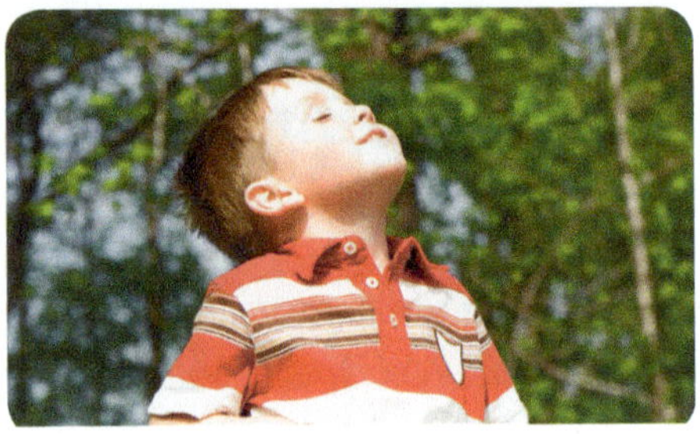

breathe

seed

soil

2 Complete the sentences.

a The seeds need ____________ and water to grow.

b Bees live in a ____________.

c The hive is in the ____________.

d We need to breathe clean ____________.

a 

b 

c 

d 

3 Match. Then complete the sentences.

1 Let's plant some ____________ in the pot.

2 Open the window! I need some ____________.

3 Let's sit under that ____________.

a tree

b seeds

c air

How do plants help us?
They clean the air.

Reading Strategy: Visualizing

When you read, you can imagine pictures in your mind.

1 Read. Use the underlined words to mark ✓ the child who is imagining the scene.

The Tree in My Yard

I have a tree,
A pretty tree
In my backyard.

My tree is full
Of yellow flowers
All summer long.

2 Read. Mark ✓ the child who is imagining the scene.

My Cat Phoebe

Phoebe loves to sleep
And play with her toys.
She loves to eat fish
And run with the boys.
Phoebe is fat.
She's a big, orange cat.
She hides in her box,
And eats all my socks!

3 Underline the words in Activity 2 that help you visualize the image.

4 Look at the illustrations on pages 150–53. What do you think the poems are about?

7.12

Mrs. Bee

By Mary C. Brooke

What are you doing, Mrs. Bee?
Collecting nectar. Look at me!
What happens then, Mrs. Bee?
I make some honey. Follow me!
Where's that honey, Mrs. Bee?
It's in my hive, up in the tree!
Can I take some honey, Mrs. Bee?
I'll sting if you do. You will see!

Think

How do bees help us?

Cows Can't Dance

By Kenn Nesbitt

If you meet
A cow by chance,
Do not ask
That cow to dance.

Cows can walk,
And cows can prance.
Cows can run,
But cows can't dance.

Cows can moo,
And munch on plants.
Cows give milk,
But cows can't dance.

So even if you
Get the chance,
Do not ask them.
Cows can't dance.

Think

What can cows do?

7.13

Five Tall Trees

By Kenn Nesbitt

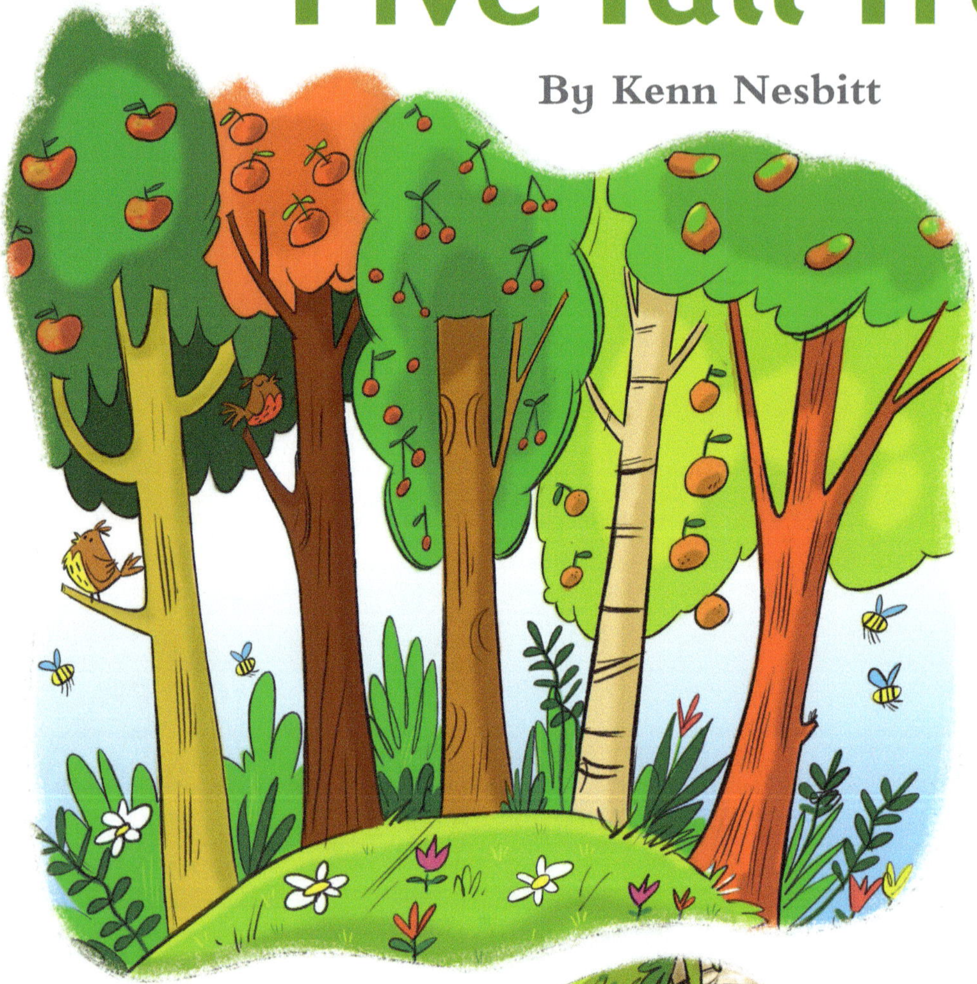

One tall tree,
One tall tree,
Grows fresh fruit
For you and me.

Two tall trees,
Two tall trees,
Make a home
For birds and bees.

Three tall trees,
Three tall trees,
Clean the **air**
That we all **breathe**.

Four tall trees,
Four tall trees,
Shade us from
The sun with ease.

Five tall trees,
Five tall trees,
Whisper secrets
In the breeze.

Think

What other animals make their home in trees?

All I Need

Unknown

All I need
For this seed
To grow
Is a little soil
In this red pot.

All I need
For this seed
To grow
Is water, sun,
And a little luck!

Think

What else do plants need to grow?

Explore the Text

1 **Circle *Yes* or *No*.**

a	Bees live in hives.	**Yes**	**No**
b	Flowers make honey.	**Yes**	**No**
c	Cows can dance.	**Yes**	**No**
d	Trees clean the air.	**Yes**	**No**
e	Seeds grow in soil.	**Yes**	**No**

2 **Circle the rhyming words.**

a	bee	nectar	make	tree	see
b	dance	chance	walk	prance	hive
c	seed	need	soil	feed	fruit

3 7.14 **Listen and check your answers.**

4 **Go back to the poem on page 153. Draw what you visualize will grow from the pot.**

How are animals and plants connected?
Some animals eat plants.

Grammar: Countable and Uncountable Nouns

Countable Nouns: a **tree**, a **bee**, a **cow**
Uncountable Nouns: some **honey**, some **soil**, some **water**

1 7.15 **Listen and number.**

2 Circle *Yes* or *No*.

a There are three apples on the table. **Yes No**
b There is some cheese on the table. **Yes No**
c There are nine eggs in the basket. **Yes No**
d There are three cucumbers in the basket. **Yes No**
e There is some butter on the table. **Yes No**

3 Look and answer. What's in the refrigerator?

There are …

a ______________________.

b ______________________.

There is …

c ______________________.

d ______________________.

Time to Talk!

Tell your partner what you have in your lunchbox.
I have some juice. I have a banana.

Listening

1 7.16 **Listen and circle *Yes* or *No*.**

Do all fruits and vegetables grow on trees? **Yes** **No**

2 7.16 **Listen again and match.**

grow on a tree

grow underground

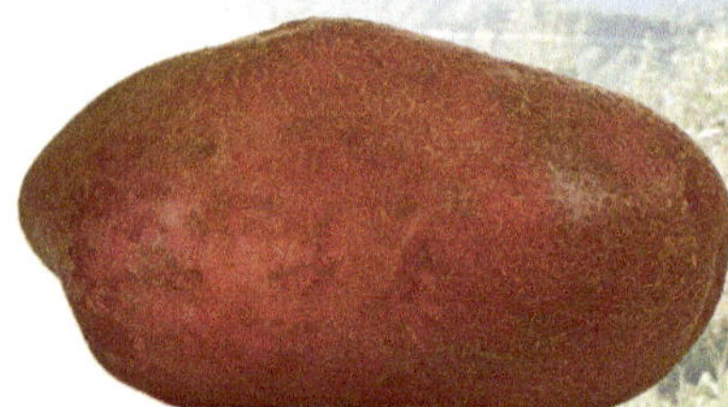

Projecting Your Voice

1 Form groups. Discuss the **Oracy Time!** topic.
2 Speak clearly and loudly.
3 Tell your classmates to speak up if you can't hear them.
4 Complete **Check Your Oracy!** in the Activity Book on page 137.

Oracy Time!

Think of two foods you can make with your favorite fruit or vegetable.
Apples are my favorite fruit. I can make apple pie and fruit salad.

Values AB page 136

How can we show where produce comes from?

Your challenge is to draw a diagram to show where produce comes from.

1. **Bring** photos of animal and plant products to class. For example, a banana, an egg, a carton of milk, etc.
2. **Collect** the photos in the center of the classroom so everybody can see them.
3. **Form** groups. Discuss where the items come from: Cows give us milk. Apples grow on trees.
4. **Draw** a diagram to show where produce comes from: seed → tree → apple
5. **Present** your diagram to the class.
6. **Speak** clearly and loudly.
7. **Tell** your classmate to speak up if you can't hear him or her.

You plant the seed in the soil. Next, the tree grows. The tree grows flowers. The flowers grow into fruit. Apples!

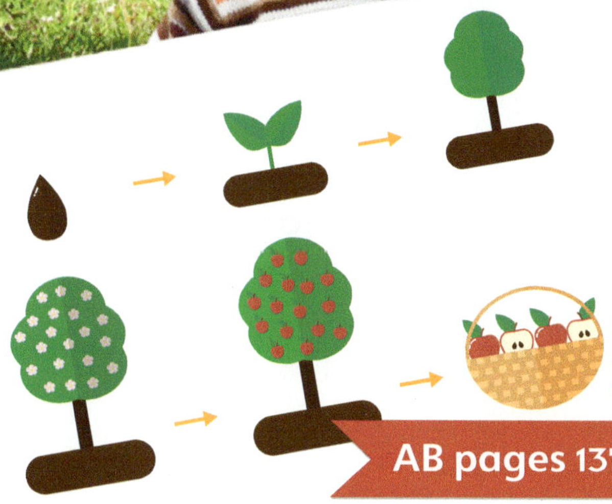

Why do we need plants and animals?
Look back through the unit. Share your ideas.

AB pages 137–39

SPEAKING MISSION

Buy vegetables at the market.

Before Your Mission

1 7.17 **Listen, look, and repeat.**

☐ **pepper**

☐ **broccoli**

☐ **onion**

☐ **beans**

☐ **lettuce**

☐ **spinach**

2 **Mark ✓ the vegetables you can use in a salad.**

3 7.18 **Listen and mark ✓. Why does Mom want to buy vegetables?**

☐ To make a salad. ☐ To make vegetable soup.

4 7.18 **Listen again. Circle the vegetables the girl and her mom buy.**

peppers broccoli onions lettuce beans spinach

Time to Talk!

Form groups. Can you name a fruit or vegetable for every color of the rainbow? **Apples are red.**

During Your Mission

5 7.18 **Listen again and mark ✓. Mom wants to make a salad for …**

☐ breakfast. ☐ lunch. ☐ dinner.

6 **Form groups. Talk about the vegetables you like.**

I like tomatoes. And you?

I like carrots.

7 **In pairs, role-play buying vegetables at a farmer's market.**

Key Language

Let's make a salad for lunch.
Let's go to the market.
Let's buy beans. I like beans!
What are these?
They're peppers.
We'll take them, too.
Is this spinach?
Yes.
We'll take spinach, too.
How much is it?
It's seven dollars, please.
Here you go.
Thank you.
Good-bye.

How do vegetables and fruit help us?
They give us energy.

8 What is imagination?

- [ ] **Talk** about things you imagine.
- [ ] **Learn** to stand up straight and speak clearly.
- [ ] **Write** a description of a picture.
- [ ] **Present** an imaginary creature.
- [ ] **Invite** friends to a costume party.

What can you see?

What do you like to create?

How do you use your imagination?

8.1

Key Words 1

painting
paintbrush
sculpture
clay
camera
photograph

1 8.1 **Watch the video. Mark ✓ the things you see.**

☐ a painting ☐ a camera ☐ a toy ☐ a sculpture
☐ a paintbrush

2 8.1 **Watch again. Complete the graphic organizer in the Activity Book.**

AB page 142

Unit 8A Ready to Read: Nonfiction

Reading Strategy: Understanding Sequence

A sequence is the steps we follow to create something.

1 **Read and number the steps.**

How to Make an Astronaut Helmet

Next, cover the box with aluminum foil.

Finally, your helmet is ready!

First, draw a big square on a large card-board box. Cut out the square.

Then, use pipe cleaners to make the antennae.

After that, decorate your helmet any way you want.

2 **Underline the sequence words in Activity 1.**

3 **Look and read. Write *First*, *Next*, *Then*, and *Finally*.**

How to Make a Family of Fish

Wrap the craft as a gift!

______

Collect the material you need.

______

Paint lines on the body of each fish.

______

Paint each stone a different color.

______

4 **Look at the pictures on pages 163–64. What do you think the text is about?**

8.2

Key Words 2

craft

dream

imagine

tape

glue

let dry

decorate

8.3

Animals of Our Imagination

Look at this animal. Is it a giraffe? Is it a tiger? No, it isn't. It's an *alebrije*!

Alebrijes are traditional Mexican **crafts**. They are very colorful. They can be red, green, purple, or all different colors. Alebrijes are imaginary animals.

Pedro Linares is the creator of alebrijes. One night, Pedro **dreams** that he is in a forest. Suddenly, he sees two strange animals: a donkey with butterfly wings, and a lion with the head of an eagle.

Pedro makes the animals. He uses cardboard and paper mache. Then, he paints their bodies using bright colors. He adds dots and lines to decorate them.

Today there are many artists who make alebrijes. Artists make alebrijes with paper mache or with wood. Some look like cats. Some look like frogs. Some look like birds.

8.4

Animals of Our Imagination

Materials:

newspaper

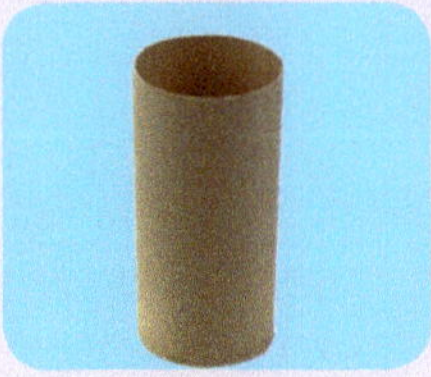
cardboard roll

glue

paint

paintbrushes

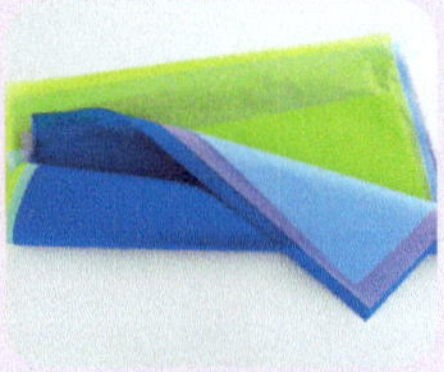
tissue paper

Steps:

1 First, close your eyes and **imagine** your alebrije.

2 Next, draw a picture of your alebrije.

3 Then, crumple newspaper to make a ball for the head. Use a cardboard roll for the body and the hooves. **Tape** the head to the body. Roll newspaper to make legs or flatten it to make wings.

4 After that, **glue** pieces of tissue paper to the body. **Let** it **dry**.

5 Paint the body. Paint the eyes and the mouth.

6 Finally, use a paintbrush and **decorate** your alebrije with lots of colors, lines, and dots!

Think

Use your imagination. What can your *alebrije* do?

My alebrije can fly!

Explore the Text

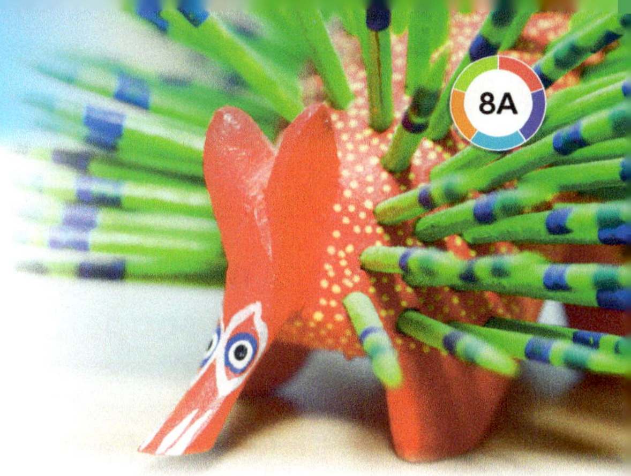

1 **Circle the correct words.**

a Alebrijes are traditional Mexican **food** / **crafts**.

b Alebrijes are imaginary **animals** / **people**.

c Pedro Linares **sees** / **dreams** about alebrijes.

2 **Look at the text on page 164.**
Complete with *First*, *Next*, *Then*, *After that*, and *Finally*.

__________, crumple newspaper to make a ball for the head. Use a cardboard roll for the body.

__________, imagine your alebrije.

__________, glue pieces of tissue paper to the body. Paint the body, the eyes, and the mouth.

__________, draw your alebrije.

__________, decorate your alebrije!

3 8.5 Key Words 3 **Listen and repeat. Number the pictures to match the meaning of *creator* and *dots*.**

1 Pedro Linares dreams about alebrijes. He is their **creator**.

2 Decorate your alebrije with lines and **dots**.

What animal combinations can you imagine?

I can imagine a horse with the body of a bee and a rabbit tail.

Grammar in Context

Grammar: Present Simple of *want* / *need*, Affirmative and Negative

She **wants** an alebrije.	She **doesn't want** a yo-yo.
We **need** newspaper.	We **don't need** plastic.

1 8.6 **Listen and match.**

Esen  Harry  Imari 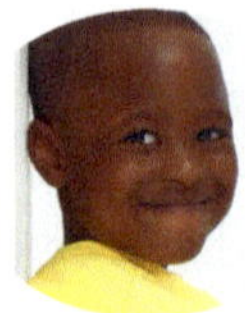 Alba 

paint

crayons

colored pencils

2 **Say what the children want and don't want.**

Esen wants colored pencils.
She doesn't want crayons.

3 8.7 **Listen. Write *need* or *needs* and match.**

1 Esen ____________ a
2 Harry ____________ a
3 Imari and Alba ____________ a

a black crayon.
b pencil sharpener.
c paintbrush.

4 **Look. Mark ✓ what you want. Cross out ✗ what you don't want.**

 ☐

kite

 ☐

bicycle

 ☐

yo-yo

 ☐

jigsaw puzzle

 ☐

roller skates

Time to Talk!

In pairs, say what you want and don't want.
I want a bicycle. I don't want a yo-yo.

1 8.8 **Listen to the story and follow.**

Cindy's Dream

By Mary C. Brooke

Cindy lives in the city.
Her house is small, but it has a big backyard.
Cindy sits in her big backyard every night.
One night, she sees a very silly sight.
A gentle giraffe walks by …
A cute camel walks by …
A giggling goose walks by, too!
Cindy is surprised and rubs her eyes.
Suddenly, she wakes up!
No more animals in her backyard …
It was all a dream!

2 8.9 **Listen and repeat the words.**

3 **Write the underlined words in Activity I in the correct column.**

Soft *c* circle	Hard *c* cup	Soft *g* gym	Hard *g* go
___	___	___	___
___	___	___	___

4 8.10 **Listen and check.**

5 8.11 **Underline the *c*'s and *g*'s. Listen. Are they hard or soft?**

a It's cold outside. Let's drink a cup of hot cocoa.
b There is a circus in the city. The ticket is one cent.
c The gate is open. The goat goes into the garden.
d Look at the giant giraffe!

Oracy

Oracy Skill: Standing Up Straight and Speaking Clearly When Giving a Presentation
When we give a presentation, we stand up straight and speak clearly.

1 8.2 **Watch the video and circle.**

1

2

a	He stands up straight and speaks clearly.	**Jack**	**Liam**
b	He moves a lot.	**Jack**	**Liam**
c	He uses expressions *This is …* and *Look at this*.	**Jack**	**Liam**

Let's Practice Oracy! 6, 7

1. Do the task in **Oracy Time!**
2. Form groups. Take turns presenting your drawing to your classmates.
3. Remember to stand up straight and speak clearly.

Oracy Time!

Draw an imaginary object or animal.

This is a special hat. When I'm mad, the hat turns red!

Check Your Oracy!

1 I presented my drawing.	**Yes / No**
2 I stood up straight and I spoke clearly.	**Yes / No**
3 I used *This is …* and *Look at this*.	**Yes / No**

Learn to Write: Adjectives

Adjectives describe places, things, and people.
My school is big.

1 Read and circle the adjectives.

1

This is a park.
It's big.
It's green.
It's beautiful.

2

This is a fish.
It's small.
It's orange and blue.
It's sad.

3

This is Hiro.
He's old.
He's thin.
He's happy.

2 Read and look. Number the pictures.

1 hot and sunny

2 heavy and gray

3 small and light

3 Choose a picture from Activity 2. Write sentences about it.

This is ______________________.

It's ______________________.

______________________.

AB pages 149–50

Unit 8B

Ready to Read: Fiction

1 8.12 Key Words 4 **Listen, look, and repeat.**

take care of

hot

tired

full

empty

thirsty

2 **Circle the correct word.**

a I'm **thirsty** / **empty**. I need some water.

b Mom is **tired** / **hot**. She needs a fan.

c Grandpa is **thirsty** / **tired**. He needs to go to bed.

d When I'm sick, Mom **plays** / **takes care of** me.

e My glass is **empty** / **full**. I want more milk.

3 **Unscramble the words. Complete the sentences.**

tyirsht oth detir

a Be careful! The pot is ____________!

b Grandma needs to go to bed. She is ____________.

c The lemonade is for Mom. She is ____________.

Time to Talk!

Say how you feel. Your partner tells you what you need.

I'm thirsty.

You need some water.

Reading Strategy: Summarizing

A summary is a short version of a text.
It includes the main idea.

1 **Read and circle.**

Gail's Flower People

Gail likes to collect petals and leaves to make imaginary people. She uses petals for the head and leaves for the body.

Summary: Gail uses petals and leaves to make imaginary people.

a Is the summary correct? **Yes No**

2 **Read. Mark ✓ the best summary.**

Todd the Doctor

Todd likes to pretend he is a doctor. He wears his father's shirt. That is his doctor's coat. He uses his mom's stethoscope. Todd plays doctor with his teddy bear.

☐ **Summary 1:** Todd plays with his teddy bear.

☐ **Summary 2:** Todd uses his imagination to pretend he is a doctor.

3 **Look at the pictures on pages 172–75. What do you think the story is about?**

What is your favorite story? Is it real or imaginary?
My favorite story is *Jack and the Beanstalk*. It's imaginary.

Remember to stand up straight and speak clearly when giving a presentation.

8.13

Ling's Paintbrush

Traditional Chinese folktale adapted by Libby Williams

Ling loves painting, but he can't paint. He does not have time. He works all day. He takes care of his cows.

One night, Ling has a dream. In his dream, he sees a woman.

The woman gives him a paintbrush. "Use this paintbrush to paint things to help people," she says.

Think

What can Ling paint with his paintbrush?

In his dream, Ling sees a boy walking under the sun. The boy is **hot** and **tired**.

Ling asks, "What do you need?"
The boy answers, "I need a place to rest and something to eat."

Ling paints a tent. He also paints a basket **full** of fruit. "Now, you can rest and eat inside the tent," says Ling.

The boy is happy now.
"Thank you, Ling," he says.

Then, Ling sees many people next to a dry river. They're holding **empty** pots. They're **thirsty**.

Ling asks, "What do you need?"
The people say, "We need water."

Ling paints a river. The people fill their pots and start drinking the water. They are happy now.
"Thank you, Ling," the people say.

Think

Why is the boy happy?
Why are the people happy?

8.14 Ling's Paintbrush

Suddenly, an old man steals the paintbrush. The old man tries to paint gold coins, but he can't.

Ling says, "You can only use the paintbrush to help people. That's why you can't paint gold coins."

The old man says, "I want gold. Gold can make me rich and happy. I am a very sad man."

"You don't need gold to be happy," says Ling.
Then, he says, "I have an idea!"

Think

What can Ling do to make the man happy?

Ling paints food.
Then, Ling and the old man give the food to people they see on the street.
The people start eating. They are happy.
"Thank you, Ling. Thank you, old man," they say.

Ling asks the old man, "Are you happy now?"
"Yes! I like helping people!" says the old man.

Ling wakes up from his dream. He feels happy.

"I helped many people in my dream. To be happy in life, I have to help real people, too!" he says.

Think

Why does Ling paint food?

Explore the Text

1 Match to complete the sentences.

1 Ling loves
2 A woman gives Ling
3 The boy needs
4 The people near the river need
5 The old man wants

a water.
b gold coins.
c painting.
d food.
e a paintbrush.

2 Mark ✓ the correct summary of *Ling's Paintbrush*.

Summary 1 ☐

The story is about a man who dreams. In his dreams, he paints things to help people.

Summary 2 ☐

The story is about an old man who is a famous painter.

3 Use the pictures to retell the story.

Imagine you have Ling's paintbrush. What can you paint?
I can paint an airplane and travel to China!

Present Simple: *want / need*; *Wh-* Questions

What does the boy need?	**He needs food.**
What do the people want?	**They want water.**

1 8.15 Listen and number the pictures.

1  **Berna**

2  **Ryan**

3  **Olivia**

4  **Ayo**

 ☐ **pail and shovel**

 ☐ **paint**

 ☐ **bike and helmet**

 ☐ **tent**

2 Ask and answer questions about the children in Activity I.

What does Berna want?

She wants some paint.

3 8.16 Listen and match.

What do the children need?

1	Karen	a	books
2	Asad	b	sweater
3	Lisa and Max	c	paintbrushes

4 Ask and answer questions about the children in Activity 3.

What does Karen need?

She needs paintbrushes.

Time to Talk!

Imagine you are at your toy store. Say what you want.
I want a new bicycle.

Listening

1 8.17 Listen. Mark ✓ what the children are imagining.

2 8.17 Listen again. Match the real objects with the imaginary ones.

a

b

c

3 As a class, discuss what other things the children can use in their game.

Standing Up Straight and Speaking Clearly

1 Do the task in **Oracy Time!**
2 Present your drawing to the class. Remember to stand up straight and speak clearly.
3 Complete **Check Your Oracy!** in the Activity Book on page 157.

Oracy Time!

Make a drawing of an imagination game you play with your friends.

Values AB page 156

How can we show what we imagine?

Your challenge is to make a painting of an imaginary animal.

1. **Draw** a sketch of your imaginary animal on a piece of white cardboard.
2. **Paint** your animal.
3. **Let** it dry.
4. **Name** your animal.
5. **Make** a list of what your imaginary animal can do.
6. **Present** your animal to the class.

This is Ziplong, my imaginary animal. It has a giraffe head, a duck body, and bird legs. It also has a chipmunk tail. It can run. It can eat leaves, too!

What is imagination?
Look back through the unit. Share your ideas.

AB pages 157–59

SPEAKING MISSION

Invite friends to a costume party.

Before Your Mission

1 8.18 **Listen, look, and repeat.**

pilot

clown

princess

superhero

cowboy

ladybug

2 You are going to a costume party. Mark ✓ the costume you want to wear.

3 8.19 **Listen and circle the costumes the children decide to wear.**

Elton

Alara

Time to Talk!

What is your favorite costume?
My favorite costume is my cowboy costume.

4 8.19 **Listen again. Circle the correct answers.**

a When is the party?

Monday Tuesday Wednesday Thursday Friday Saturday Sunday

b What time is the party?

3 p.m. 4 p.m. 5 p.m. 6 p.m.

c Where is the party?

At Trish's house At Grandma's house At school

During Your Mission

5 In pairs, role-play a conversation. Invite your friend to a costume party.

Key Language

Do you want to come to my costume party?

Sure! When is it?

It's on (Wednesday).

What time is it?

It's at (4 p.m.).

Where is it?

At (my grandma's house).

Can I go as a …?

What imagination games can you play at parties?
We can play being superheroes.

9

Why do we need clothes?

- [ ] **Learn** why we need clothes.
- [ ] **Give** and respond to positive feedback.
- [ ] **Write** about how people are doing things.
- [ ] **Learn** to classify clothes based on the weather.
- [ ] **Talk** about clothes for different occasions.

Which clothes are for playing sports?

Which clothes are for sleeping?

Which clothes protect you from the weather?

Key Words 1

clothes	dress
tennis shoes	sweater
wear	jeans

1 9.1 **Watch the video. Mark ✓ the clothes that appear.**

☐ jeans ☐ tennis shoes ☐ hat ☐ T-shirt

☐ sunglasses ☐ sweater

2 9.1 **Watch again. Complete the graphic organizer in the Activity Book.**

AB page 162

Unit 9A

Ready to Read: Nonfiction

Reading Strategy: Text-to-Self Connections

When you read a text, you can think about how it is similar to your life.

1 Read and mark ✓ the child who is making connections to his or her life.

Squirrels are rodents. They climb trees. Squirrels can live almost anywhere. You can even see them climbing trees in the park!

I go to the park with my dad every weekend. There are many animals in the park. I feed the squirrels! ☐

I go to the park with my dad every weekend. I play on the slides. I wear my favorite T-shirt. ☐

2 Read the text and make connections to your life.

Lucy is only seven years old, and she is a famous artist!

She loves to paint with her hands. You can find her paintings in art galleries or on the Internet. Many people buy her paintings!

Lucy	Me
a Lucy is seven years old.	I am ____________________.
b Lucy loves to paint.	I love to ____________________.

3 Look at pages 185–86. What do you think the text is about?

9.2

Key Words 2

sunny

cold

windy

rainy

snowy

gloves

scarf

9.3

All Year Long

This is a photo album of Canada. Canada is a big country in North America.

This is Canada in the spring. It rains a lot, so flowers bloom and plants grow. Birds make their nests and lay eggs.

Look! It's raining now! Ed is wearing his raincoat. In the spring in Canada, don't go out without your umbrella!

This is Canada in the summer. Summer comes after spring. The weather is sunny and hot.

The leaves on the trees are green. Many trees have fruit.

Some children are in the park. They are riding their bikes. It is the time of year to wear light clothes, like shorts and T-shirts!

Think

How are spring and summer different?

9.4

All Year Long

This is Canada in the fall. Fall comes after summer. The weather is a little bit cold and windy. It is rainy, too. The leaves on the trees turn yellow, brown, and red.

Some birds, like ducks and geese, fly away.

In the park, the children are walking on the leaves.

Look at the squirrel! It's collecting nuts for the winter.

This is Canada in the winter. The weather is very cold and snowy!

It is very cold outside. In the city of Montreal, people like to stay inside. They go shopping underground!

Look at the park! The trees have no leaves. Some children are building a snowman. They're wearing their winter clothes, like jackets, gloves, and scarves. Children love to play in the snow, but it is important to stay warm!

Think

Which clothes can you wear in any season?

1 **Circle *Yes* or *No*.**

a Spring is rainy in Canada. **Yes** **No**

b Summer comes after fall. **Yes** **No**

c In Canada, the leaves turn yellow, brown, and red in the fall. **Yes** **No**

d In Canada, the winter is very cold and snowy. **Yes** **No**

2 **Make connections with the text and where you live.**

In Canada, ...	Where I live, ...
it rains a lot in the spring. Flowers bloom and plants grow. Children wear their raincoats.	it ______________ in the spring. I wear ______________.
it is very cold and snowy in the winter. Children wear jackets, gloves, and scarves.	it ______________ in the winter. I wear ______________.

3 9.5 Key Words 3 **Listen and repeat. Number the pictures.**

1 In the winter, it's important to stay <u>warm</u>.

2 In the spring, flowers are in <u>bloom</u>.

What is your favorite season? Why?

My favorite season is spring.
I like to play in the park.

Grammar in Context

Grammar: Present Progressive, Affirmative and Negative

Affirmative	Negative
I'm wearing a sweater.	**I'm not wearing a scarf.**
He's wearing a raincoat.	**He isn't wearing a hat.**
The children are riding their bikes.	**The children aren't playing in the park.**

1 9.6 **Listen and number.**

1 Pam　　2 Kelly and Kay　　3 Aki

2 Circle the correct word.

a Pam **is / isn't** swinging in the park.

b Kelly and Kay **are / aren't** wearing shorts.

c Aki **is / isn't** flying kites.

d Kelly and Kay **are / aren't** wearing hats.

3 9.7 **Listen and match.**

1 Nora　　2 Emir　　3 Layla

4 With a partner, say what the children in Activity 3 are and aren't doing.

Nora is eating an apple.

She isn't riding a bike.

1 9.8 **Listen and follow.**

Sherry's Shoes
Sherry's **sh**oes are on the **sh**elf,
On the **sh**elf, on the **sh**elf.
Sherry's **sh**oes are on the **sh**elf,
And **sh**e can't reach them!

The Funny Chimpanzee
Charlie is a **ch**impanzee,
Chimpanzee, **ch**impanzee.
He's a funny **ch**impanzee,
And **ch**ildren love him!

2 9.9 **Listen and repeat the words with the *sh* and *ch* sounds.**

sh	Sherry	shoes	shelf	she
ch	Charlie	chimpanzee	children	

3 9.10 **Listen and match.**

sh ***ch***

1 

2 

3 

4 

4 9.11 **Listen, read, and repeat the tongue twisters. In pairs, say them as fast as you can.**

There's a seashell by the seashore.

Chuck chooses cheese and cherries.

Oracy Skill: Giving and Responding to Positive Feedback
We can give and respond to positive feedback.

1 9.2 9.12 **Watch and circle the correct answer or answers.**

a Who gives positive feedback? **Emma Jack Kate**

b Who receives positive feedback? **Emma Jack Kate**

2 9.2 9.12 **Watch again and circle the phrases you hear.**

Thank you! | Great job! | Speak up, please. | Nice drawing!

Let's Practice Oracy! 14, 15, 16

1. Do the **Oracy Time!** task.
2. Form groups. Present your drawing to your group.
3. Give positive feedback to your classmates.

Oracy Time!

Draw yourself wearing your favorite clothes.

These are my favorite tennis shoes.

Check Your Oracy!

1 I spoke clearly and loudly.	Yes / No
2 My classmates gave me positive feedback.	Yes / No
3 I said, "Thank you!"	Yes / No

Learn to Write: Adverbs

An adverb tells how an action happens.

The squirrel is running quickly. **The children are walking slowly.**

1 Read and circle the adverbs.

In this photo, my brother and I are running happily through a field. The wind is blowing softly. After a long winter, spring is here! The flowers are growing quickly.

2 Read and answer the questions.

a How are the children running? ________________.

b How is the wind blowing? ________________.

c How are the flowers growing? ________________.

3 Look and describe what the children are doing. Use adverbs.

(speak / loud)

(play / happy)

____

____

(read / quiet)

____

I jump rope slowly! How about you?

AB pages 169–70

Ready to Read: Fiction

1 9.13 Key Words 4 **Listen, look, and repeat.**

pants

boots

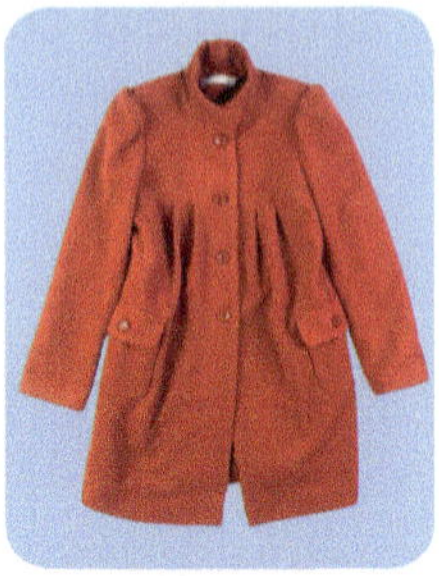
coat

pocket

take off

put on

2 **Read and complete. Use words from Activity I.**

Marlon loves his purple ________.

He wears it every day, even when it's hot!

He ________ it ______ in the morning.

He only ________ it ______ at night.

His coat has two ____________.

What do you think he keeps inside them?

3 **Match the questions with the answers.**

1 What do you wear when it's cold outside?

2 Do you have a coat?

a No, I don't. I have a jacket.

b I wear pants, boots, and a sweater.

4 **Work in pairs. Ask a partner the questions in Activity 3.**

What do you keep in your pockets?
I have a toy car and a piece of candy.

Reading Strategy: Main Idea and Details

The main idea is what the story is about.
Details tell us more about the main idea.

1 **Read. Underline the main idea.**

The Storm

It looks like the storm is here! Big drops of rain are falling. The sky is full of purple and black clouds. The thunder is getting louder and louder. The lightning makes the sky shine brightly!

Main Idea

a Lightning makes the sky shine brightly.

b Big drops of rain are falling.

c There is a big storm outside.

d The thunder is getting louder.

2 **Write three details about the text in Activity 1.**

1 Detail

____

____

____

2 Detail

____

____

____

3 Detail

____

____

____

3 **You are going to read a story on pages 194–97. What do you think the story is about?**

9.14

Nasreddin and the Party

Adapted from a Turkish folktale by Caroline Linse

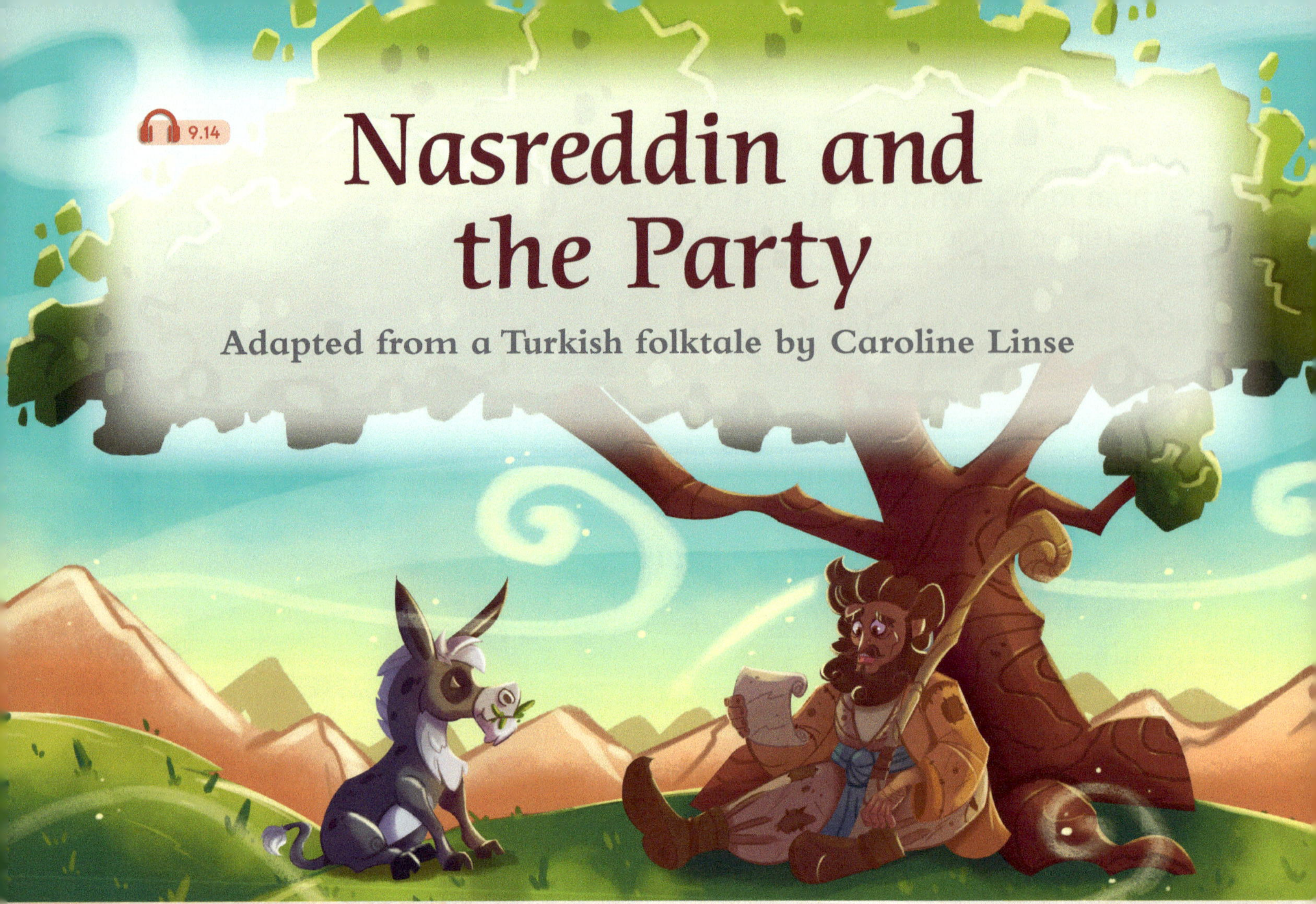

It is a beautiful day in the countryside.
The sun is shining. The wind is blowing lightly. Nasreddin, a merchant, is with his donkey. He is sitting under a tree. The donkey is munching some grass.

Nasreddin is wearing his favorite clothes: an old shirt, old **pants**, a pair of old **boots**, and an old **coat**. They are old, but they are comfortable.

Suddenly, Nasreddin puts his hand in his coat **pocket**. He finds a piece of paper.
"What's this?" he asks.
"Oh, no!" he says. "This is an invitation to Hassan's party! It's today!"

Nasreddin feels nervous. He wants to go to the party, but it's late. He can't go home and change his clothes.

Think

Why is Nasreddin going to the party in his old clothes?

Nasreddin gets to Hassan's home and knocks at the door.
"Hello, Hassan," says Nasreddin, smiling.
Hassan is happy to see Nasreddin, but then he looks at his clothes.

"Why are you wearing these clothes, Nasreddin? These are not party clothes," he says.
"I know," says Nasreddin, "let me explain."

Hassan looks at Nasreddin's old clothes again and turns away.
He doesn't let Nasreddin explain. He doesn't ask him to come in.

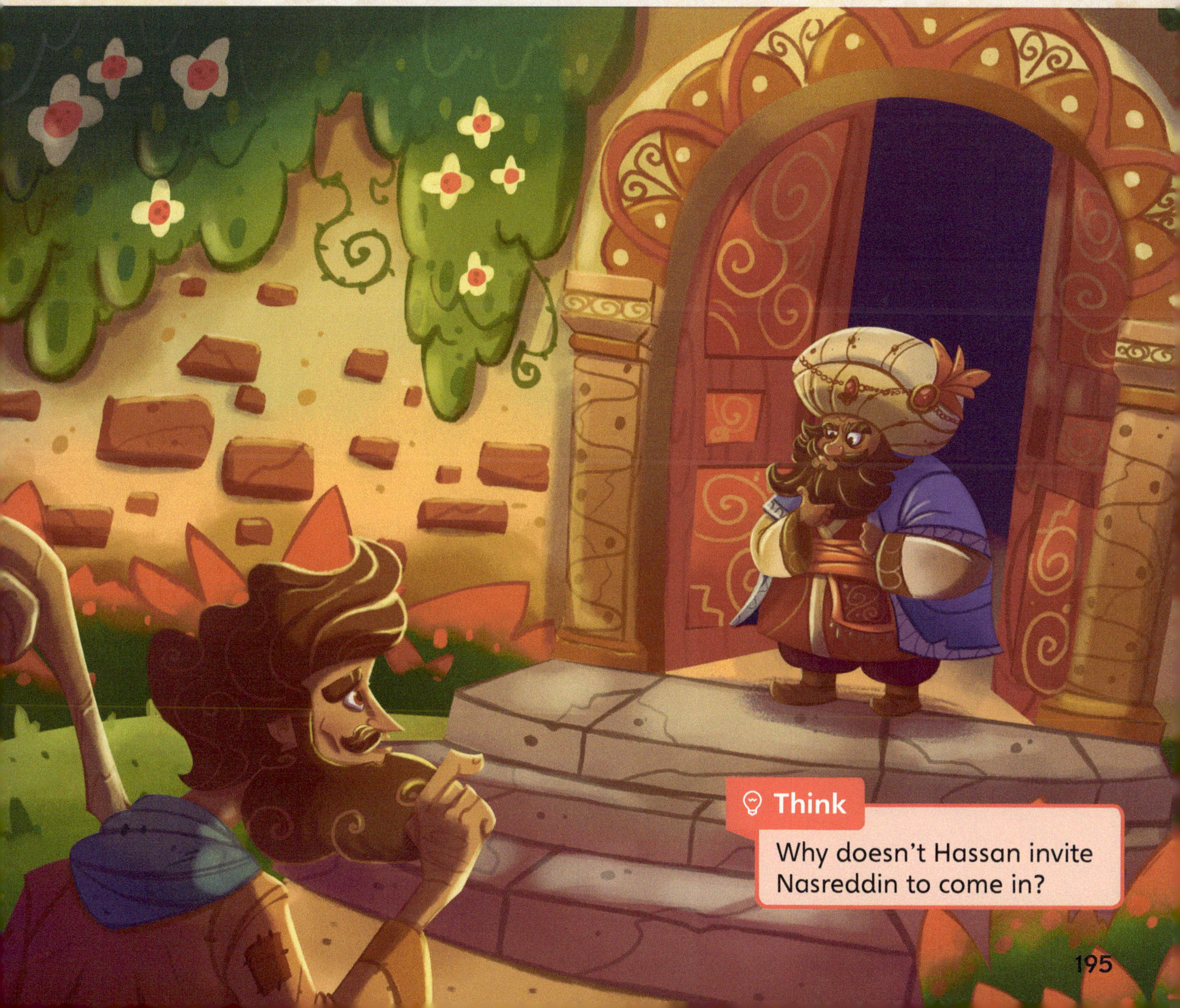

Think

Why doesn't Hassan invite Nasreddin to come in?

9.15

Nasreddin and the Party

Nasreddin gets on his donkey and goes back home.
When he gets home, Nasreddin takes off his old clothes. He puts on new clothes: a new shirt, new pants, a new pair of boots, and a new coat. Nasreddin is not happy, but he goes back to the party.

He knocks at Hassan's door again. Hassan answers the door. He looks at Nasreddin's new clothes and smiles. "Come in, my dear friend!" Hassan says.

Think

Nasreddin is not happy. Why does he go back to the party?

Nasreddin comes in. He goes with his friend Hassan to the dining room.

Hassan asks Nasreddin to sit at the table.
"Sit, please, dear friend," says Hassan.
Nasreddin takes off his coat and puts it on the chair.
"Eat, coat, eat!" he says.
Hassan is shocked.

"What are you doing, Nasreddin?" asks Hassan.
"I'm inviting my coat to eat," says Nasreddin. "My coat is welcome at your party. I'm not welcome! You like my clothes. You don't like me!"

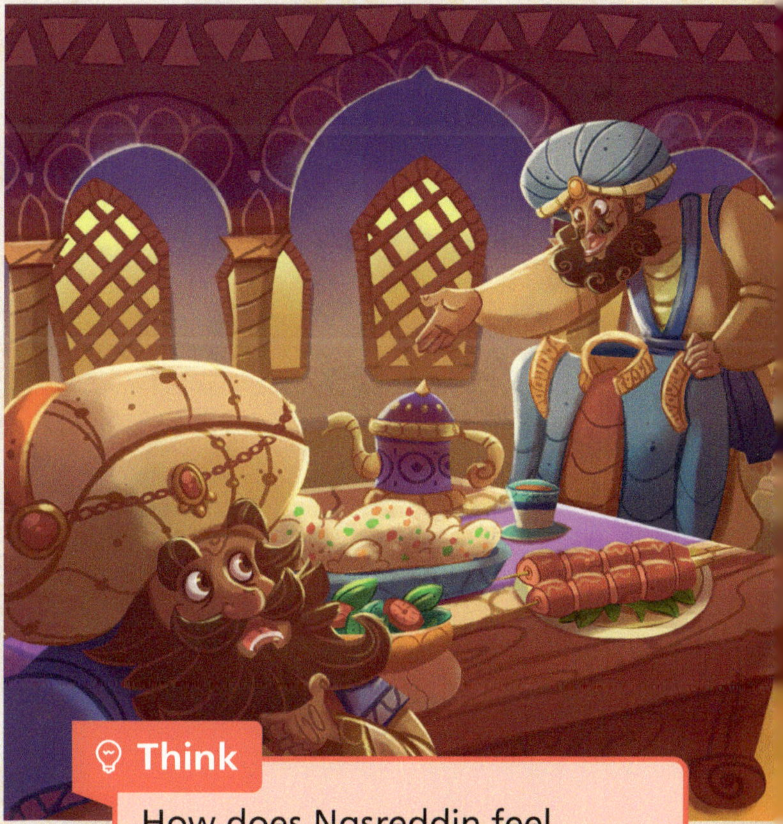

Think

How does Nasreddin feel about his friend: angry or sad? Why does he feel that way?

Explore the Text

1 Circle *Yes* or *No*.

a Nasreddin has an invitation to a party. **Yes No**

b First, Nasreddin goes to the party wearing his old clothes. **Yes No**

c Hassan likes Nasreddin's old clothes. **Yes No**

d Nasreddin eats at the party. He is happy. **Yes No**

2 Read. Circle *Main Idea* or *Detail*.

a Nasreddin has a donkey. **Main Idea Detail**

b Nasreddin thinks friends are more important than clothes. **Main Idea Detail**

c Nasreddin asks his coat to eat at the party. **Main Idea Detail**

3 Number the pictures. Then, retell the story with a partner.

What clothes do you wear on special occasions?

I wear pants and a sweater.

I wear a dress.

Remember to give and respond to positive feedback.

Grammar: Present Progressive, *Yes/No* Questions

Is Nasreddin **sitting** under a tree? **Yes**, he **is**.
Are the people at the party **dancing**? **No**, they **aren't**.

1 9.16 **Listen. Who is Cindy? Mark ✓ the correct girl.**

2 Write the correct answer.

a Is Cindy wearing a dress? ______________________.

b Is she eating cake? ______________________.

c Are Sam and Cindy playing ball? ______________________.

3 Choose a child from the picture. Ask and answer questions with a partner.

Is it a boy or a girl?

It's a boy.

Is he talking to Cindy?

No, he isn't.

Time to Talk!

Tell a partner where you are. Your partner guesses what you are wearing.

I'm at the park.
Are you wearing pants and a sweater?
No. I'm wearing shorts and a T-shirt.

1 9.17 **Listen and circle the correct word.**

Uncle Rob is a …

teacher

farmer

nurse

2 9.17 **Listen again. Mark ✓ the clothes Ken needs to pack.**

Packing List

jeans ☐	shorts ☐	socks ☐	cap ☐
tennis shoes ☐	jacket ☐	gloves ☐	boots ☐
T-shirts ☐	sweater ☐	hat ☐	scarf ☐

3 **With a partner, discuss why Ken needs to pack his boots and hat.**

Giving and Responding to Positive Feedback

1 Do the **Oracy Time!** task.
2 Form groups. Show your drawing to your group.
3 Give positive feedback to your classmates.
4 Complete **Check Your Oracy!** in the Activity Book on page 177.

Oracy Time!

Draw yourself wearing your favorite clothes and doing your favorite free-time activity.

Values AB page 176

How can we choose clothes for different types of weather?

Your challenge is to classify clothing items according to the weather.

1. **Brainstorm** different clothing items for the following types of weather: sunny, rainy, windy, and snowy.
2. **Draw** the clothing items on white sheets of paper.
3. **Cut out** the clothing items and paste them onto construction paper squares to make cards.
4. **Make** four small cardboard boxes: one for each type of weather.
5. **Label** the boxes: *sunny*, *rainy*, *windy*, and *snowy*. You can draw a picture for each box.
6. **Put** the cards with the different clothing items into the corresponding boxes.
7. **Present** your boxes and cards to your group.

When it's snowy, I wear pants, socks, boots, and a coat.

Why do we need clothes? Look back through the unit. Share your ideas.

AB pages 177–79

Oracy Performance Task 3: Presentation

1 Read and match.

1 When you project your voice,
2 When you stand up straight,
3 When you give your classmates positive feedback,

a they feel confident.
b your classmates can hear you.
c your classmates can see you.

2 In pairs, match the pictures with the language.

YOUR TASK

You are invited to go camping, to a fancy party, and to a sports event.

The three events are on the same day at the same time.

Your task is to decide where to go and what to wear.

I want to go ...

camping.

to a fancy party.

to a sports event.

I want to wear ...

tennis shoes.

a shirt.

jeans.

a jacket.

a T-shirt.

pants.

a cap.

shoes.

a dress and a sweater.

1. Decide where you want to go. Circle the clothes you want to wear.
2. Make a drawing showing where you are going and what you are wearing.
3. Form groups. Present your drawing to your group. Remember to stand up straight and speak clearly.
4. Give positive feedback to your classmates.

Check Your Oracy!

	☺	☺☺	☺☺☺
1 I stood up straight.			
2 I spoke clearly.			
3 I gave positive feedback.			
4 I responded to positive feedback.			

adopt *verb* to take an animal that your family can keep

air *noun* the gases that we breathe but cannot see

ant *noun* a very small insect that lives in groups under the ground

apartment *noun* a set of rooms for one family in a building

art room *noun* a room in a school where you draw and paint

artisan *noun* someone who makes things using a lot of skill

aunt *noun* the sister of your mom or dad, or the woman who is married to your uncle

backyard *noun* the land behind a house

bake cookies *verb phrase* to make a small sweet food that you cook in an oven

basket *noun* a container that you carry or keep things in, usually made of thin pieces from plants

bedtime *noun* the time when you get into your bed so you can sleep

bee *noun* a flying insect that is yellow and black

bloom *verb* to make flowers

boot *noun* a kind of shoe that covers your foot and the lower part of your leg

break *verb* to make something into two or more pieces and damage it

breathe *verb* to move air into and out of your body through your nose and mouth

bring *verb* to take something to a place or a person

brother *noun* a boy or man who has the same parents as you

butterfly *noun* a flying insect with large colored wings

buy *verb* to pay money for something so you can keep it

cafeteria *noun* the place in a school where you go to eat

calf *noun* a baby cow

call *verb* to use a phone to try to talk to someone

camera *noun* a machine you use to take photographs

catch *verb* to use your hand to stop something that is moving through the air and start to hold it

cave *noun* a large hole in the side of a mountain

chat *verb* to talk to someone in a friendly way

cheese *noun* a food made from milk, hard or soft, usually yellow or white

chipmunk *noun* a small animal with fur and stripes on its back that lives in holes in the ground

choose *verb* to decide what you want from two or more things

chore *noun* work you have to do at home

classmate *noun* someone who is in the same class as you

classroom *noun* a room in a school for a teacher and students

clay *noun* a kind of soft, wet dirt that becomes hard when you dry or bake it

clean *adjective* not having any dirt, food, or marks on something

clean up *phrasal verb* to make a place neat by putting things in the right places

cloth *noun* a material used to make clothes, sheets for a bed, and many other things

clothes *noun* things that you put on your body to cover it, such as a dress, pants, or shirt

coat *noun* something you wear over your other clothes to keep warm

cold *adjective* not hot and having a low temperature

collect *verb* to get and keep many things of one kind because you like them

computer lab *noun* a room in a school where there are computers

cousin *noun* the child of your aunt or uncle

craft *noun* something that you make with your hands, especially a work of art

creator *noun* someone who has made something new

crop *noun* plants that are grown on a farm or in a garden so that we can eat them

dance *verb* to move your body and feet to music

decorate *verb* to make something look pretty by adding color or other things to it

desk *noun* a table that you can work at

dig *verb* to move dirt and make a hole

dirty *adjective* having dirt, food, or marks that should not be there

donate *verb* to give things you do not use anymore to a store or a group to help them

dot *noun* a very small round mark

dragonfly *noun* an insect with a long colored body and four thin wings

draw pictures *verb phrase* to use a pen, pencil, or crayon on paper to show what something looks like

drawing *noun* a picture you make using a pen, pencil, or crayon

dream *verb* to see pictures and stories in your mind when you are sleeping

dress *noun* something a woman or girl wears that covers the top part of her body and hangs down over her legs

earthworm *noun* a living thing with no legs that lives in the ground

egg *noun* a food that comes from chickens. It has a hard shell and is yellow and white inside.

empty *adjective* not having anything inside

evening *noun* the time between the end of the day and the beginning of the night

family *noun* your mom, dad, brothers, sisters, grandparents, uncles, aunts, and cousins

father *noun* a male parent; a dad

find *verb* to look for something and see where it is

fish *noun* an animal that lives in water and has no legs

fit *verb* to be the right size or shape to put on or in something

flower *noun* a part of a plant that is colored and pretty and often smells nice

fly *verb* to move through the air

fly kites *verb phrase* to make a flat toy called a kite go up into the air

forest *noun* a large area of land with many trees and plants and no buildings

friend *noun* someone you like a lot and have fun with and who will help you

frog *noun* a small animal that lives in water and on land and has strong legs for jumping

full *adjective* having a lot of things inside, so nothing more can go in

gift *noun* something that you give someone to keep

glove *noun* something you wear on your hand

glue *verb* to join things together using a sticky liquid called glue

goat *noun* an animal that has horns and hair that hangs down from its chin and lives on a farm

grandfather *noun* the father of your mom or dad; a grandpa

grandmother *noun* the mother of your mom or dad; a grandma

grandparent *noun* the father or mother of your mom or dad

grass *noun* a plant with thin green leaves that covers the ground

gym *noun* a large room inside a school where you play sports

happy *adjective* feeling good

hare *noun* a big rabbit that can run very fast and has long ears

helicopter *noun* an aircraft that has wings on top that go around very fast

help *verb* to do work that makes it easier for someone else to do something

hive *noun* a thing that bees live in

homework *noun* work that you do at home for school

hot *adjective* having a lot of heat, for example, from the sun or a fire

hound *noun* a kind of dog used for hunting

house *noun* a building that a family lives in

imagine *verb* to make a picture or idea in your mind when you are awake

inside *preposition* in something like a box or building

jam *noun* a sweet, soft food made by cooking fruit with sugar

jeans *noun* pants made of thick strong cloth. Jeans are often blue.

jump rope *verb phrase* to use your legs to push yourself into the air and over a long rope that you are moving over your head and under your feet

kind *noun* a group of things that are the same in some ways

let dry *verb phrase* to allow something the time it needs to become dry and not wet

library *noun* a room or building with a lot of books that people can read

list *noun* a set of words, names, or things that you write down in order, one after another

listen to music *verb phrase* to hear songs or musical instruments

make *verb* to do something with things so that there is something new when you are done

make the bed *verb phrase* to pull up the covers on a bed and make it look neat

math *noun* the study of numbers and shapes

meat *noun* a food that is made from an animal, for example, a cow or sheep

mosquito *noun* a small flying insect that bites people and animals and sucks their blood

mother *noun* a female parent; a mom

music room *noun* a room in a school where you learn about and play music

naughty *adjective* behaving badly and not doing what you are told to do

neighbor *noun* someone who lives near you

new *adjective* used for the first time

nurse *noun* someone whose job is to care for people who are sick or hurt

old *adjective* not new

outside *preposition* not in something like a box or building

paint *verb* to make a picture using colored liquids called paints

paintbrush *noun* a brush you use to put paint on a picture or wall

painting *noun* a picture that you make with a colored liquid called paint

pajamas *noun* clothes you wear in bed

pants *noun* something you wear with two parts to cover your legs

parent *noun* your mom or dad

park *noun* a large area of land with grass and trees and places to play

pet *noun* an animal that you keep at your house

photograph *noun* a picture that you make using a camera

pick up *phrasal verb* to use your hand to lift something from a surface like the floor or a table

play games *verb phrase* to do a fun activity that you try to win

play soccer *verb phrase* to kick a ball to another person or into a goal

pocket *noun* a place in your clothes where you can put small things

pond *noun* a small area of water where fish or plants can live

principal *noun* someone whose job is to be the leader of a school

pull *verb* to move something toward you

puppet *noun* a toy that looks like a person or animal. You can put your hand inside it or move it with strings.

push *verb* to move something away from you

put on *phrasal verb* to make your clothes go onto your body

rainy *adjective* with a lot of water falling from the sky

ram *noun* a male sheep

read stories *verb phrase* to look at the words and pictures in a book and understand them

reading *noun* a subject in school or an activity in which you look at words and understand them

recess *noun* the time at school when you can play

recycle *verb* to put old paper, bottles, and cans into a special box so they can be taken away and made into other things

rest *verb* to sit or lie down but not sleep

ride bikes *verb phrase* to sit on a bike and use your feet to make it move

run away *phrasal verb* to escape from a place or person

sad *adjective* feeling bad and crying or wanting to cry

same *adjective* not a different place, person, or thing

scarf *noun* something you wear around your neck to keep warm

school *noun* a place where children go to learn things

sculpture *noun* a work of art made from wood, clay, metal, or stone

see *verb* to use your eyes to notice the things around you

seed *noun* a small thing that a new plant grows from

set the table *verb phrase* to put plates, glasses, and things you eat with on the table before a meal

share *verb* to use something with someone else at the same time

sing songs *verb phrase* to use your voice and words to make music

sister *noun* a girl or woman who has the same parents as you

sleep *verb* to lie down with your eyes closed and not be thinking or moving

slide *noun* a thing you play on by climbing to the top and then sitting down and moving to the bottom

snack *noun* a food you eat between meals, for example, fruit

snowy *adjective* with a lot of frozen water falling from the sky

soil *noun* the dirt that plants grow in

sunny *adjective* having a lot of light from the sun

sweater *noun* something you wear on the top part of your body to keep you warm

sweep the floor *verb phrase* to clean a floor with a large brush called a broom

swing *noun* a seat that hangs from a bar or a tree. You sit on the seat and move backward and forward in the air.

tadpole *noun* a baby frog. Tadpoles live in water and have a big head and a long tail.

tail *noun* a part of an animal's body that sticks out from its bottom

take care *verb phrase* to give someone the things he or she needs to stay safe or healthy

take off *phrasal verb* to make your clothes come off your body

tape *verb* to use pieces of thin sticky material to join two things together

teacher *noun* someone whose job is to help students learn in a school

tennis shoes *noun* shoes with a soft bottom that you wear to play sports

tent *noun* a house made of cloth that you can move from place to place

thirsty *adjective* needing to drink

tidy *adjective* having everything in the right place

tie *verb* to fasten together two ends of a piece of string

tired *adjective* feeling like you want to go to sleep

trash *noun* things that have been used and are not needed anymore

travel *verb* to go to another place

tree *noun* a tall plant with a trunk, branches, and leaves

uncle *noun* the brother of your mom or dad, or the man who is married to your aunt

uniform *noun* clothes that everyone in a school or job wears

wake up *phrasal verb* to stop sleeping

warm *adjective* not too hot and not cold

water lily *noun* a plant that grows on top of water and has big, flat leaves and flowers

water the plants *verb phrase* to pour water on plants to keep them alive

wear *verb* to have clothes on your body

windy *adjective* with a lot of moving air

wood *noun* the hard substance that trees are made of

write *verb* to make words or numbers, for example, with a pen or computer

writing *noun* a subject in school or an activity in which you use a pen or pencil to make words or stories